GASTRIC BYPASS COOKBOOK

125+ QUICK AND EASY, DELICIOUS, AND HEALTHY RECIPES FOR AFTER WEIGHT-LOSS SURGERY. TAKE CARE OF YOUR NEW STOMACH

Ronda M. Martin

TABLE OF CONTENT

Chapter 1: Gastric bypass surgery 6
Gastric Bypass Guide 6
Benefits 6
WHY IT'S DONE 7
WHO IT'S FOR 7
HOW DO YOU PREPARE? 8
WHERE CAN YOU EXPECT IT? 8

Chapter 2 : Stage 1: diet and tips 10
1. fat-free chicken broth 10
2. LOW-FAT VEGETABLE BROTH 10
3. KETO SUGAR-FREE RASPBERRY JELLO CUPS 11

SATGE 2: FULL LIQUIDS / PUREED FOODS RECIPES & TIPS. 12
1. Orange Creamsicle Protein Smoothie 12
2. low carb green smoothie 12
3. mango pevery smoothie 13
4. pineapple coconut smoothie 14
5. watermelon strawberry protein smoothie 15
6. ROOT VEGETABLE SOUP 15
7. GARLIC AND VEGETABLE SOUP 16
8. chicken clear soup 17
9. Fluffy Egg White Omelette 18
10. Protein Chai Latte with Coconut Milk Froth 19
11. chocolate protein shake 20
12. easy egg custard 21
13. creamy healthy soup 21
14. PUMPKIN CARROT SOUP 23
15. PUREED CLASSIC EGG SALAD 24
16. blueberry lemonade vitamin smoothie 25
17. strawberry greek yogurt whip 26
18. eggnog protein shake 27
19. creamy carrot and ginger soup 28
20. Classic Tomato Soup 29
21. mexican egg puree 30
22. chimichurri chicken puree 31
23. Ground Turkey Burritos With Refried Beans 31
24. chicken and black bean mole puree 33
25. PUMPKIN PIE PROTEIN SHAKE 34
26. gingerbread cookie protein shake 35
27. lemon garlic pureed salmon 36
28. SINGLE-SERVE BAKED RICOTTA 37
29. creamy shrimp scampi 38
30. CHOCOLATE PEANUT BUTTER PROTEIN SHAKE 39
31. Low-fat refried beans 40
32. Pumpkin Curry Soup with Chicken 41
33. Roasted Red Pepper & Black Bean Enchiladas 43
34. green protein smoothie 44
35. white bean soup 45
36. carrot lemonde smoothie 46
37. Silky Sweet Potato Puree 47

38.	Buffalo-Ranch Slow-Cooker Chicken	47
39.	chili puree	48
40.	no chew cheeseburgers	49
41.	italian chicken puree	50
42.	Creamy Ricotta and White Bean Dip	50
43.	ginger garlic tofu puree	51
44.	moroccan fish puree	52
45.	sesame tuna salad puree	53
46.	caribbean pork puree	54
47.	rosemary chicken with blue cheese	55
48.	mediterranean chicken puree	56
49.	pureed chicken salad	57
50.	chicken and sweet potato puree	57
51.	Banana, Tofu + Pear Baby Food Puree	59
52.	cheesy cauliflower puree	59
53.	basic oatmeal	60
54.	peppermint Milkshake	61
55.	Lemon crystl shake	61
56.	orange tea	62
57.	PUREED VEGETABLE	63

Stage 3: Semi-solid/soft foods ... 65

1.	high protein deviled egg and bacon	65
2.	baked ricotta florentine	66
3.	spinach soup with lemon	67
4.	Pulled Pork Taco Soup	68
5.	greek yogurt parfait	69
6.	banana spinach protein smoothie	70
7.	mocha java	70
8.	berry avocado smoothie	71
9.	tuscan white bean soup	72
10.	Chocolate Cherry Smoothie	74
11.	turkey kale meatballs	75
12.	buffalo chicken meatballs	76
13.	Ricotta scrambled eggs	77
14.	zucchini soup	78
15.	Slow Cooker Chicken Curry	79
16.	baked fish with almond chutney	81
17.	CRANBERRY, SAGE, AND GRUYERE TURKEY MEATBALLS	82
18.	juice jelly / jello pots	83
19.	spinach and feta bake	84
20.	soft card salad	85
21.	spicy vegetarian chili	86
22.	Avocado Chicken Power Salad	88
23.	taco casserole	88
24.	Summer Vegetables with Sausage and Potatoes Skillet	90
25.	strawberry oatmeal bars	91
26.	pina colada protein shake	92
27.	High Protein Creamy Taco Soup	93
28.	pumpkin spice hot chocolate	94
29.	African Chicken Peanut Stew	95
30.	scotch eggs	96
31.	Low-Carb, High-Protein Egg Salad	97
32.	smoked salmon pate	98

33.	crustless Quiche	99
34.	PEANUT BUTTER PROTEIN BARS	101
35.	swede soup	102
36.	chili lime turkey burgers	104
37.	cranberry chicken salad	105
38.	ITALIAN MEATLOAF	106
39.	creamy tuscan shrimp	107
40.	CHEESY CHICKEN AND BROCCOLI CASSEROLE	108
41.	cauliflower "fried Rice"	109
42.	BACON AND VEGETABLE SOUP	111
43.	instant pot turkey chili	112
44.	Crockpot Chicken Taco Chili	113
45.	turkey meatloaf	114
46.	granola bar	115
47.	COCOA ALMOND PROTEIN SMOOTHIE	116
48.	HASHBROWN EGG CASSEROLE	117
49.	lemon garlic salmon	118
Stgate 4: fish and seafood recipes		**119**
1.	Crispy Garlic Parmesan Salmon	119
2.	coconut fish curry	120
3.	dijon baked salmon	121
4.	Salmon Patties With Dill Sauce	122
5.	seared scallops and cauliflower rice risotto	123
6.	seafood chowder	124
7.	CASHEW , CHILLI, AND LIME CRUSTED FISH	125
8.	tandoori salmon	126
9.	asian shrimp and brussels sprouts	127
10.	brazilian fish stew	129
11.	SCRAMBLED EGGS WITH SMOKED SALMON	130
12.	fish taco blows	131
13.	Creamy Fish Fillet Casserole	132
14.	Soy Ginger Salmon	133
15.	HALIBUT CEVICHE	135
16.	Baked Pesto Salmon	136

INTRODUCTION

Gastric bypass surgery is a medical procedure that can help obese people lose weight and improve their health. It causes the stomach to shrink and changes the way the stomach and small intestine absorb food, making weight loss easier. In addition, this procedure is known as a Roux-en-Y gastric bypass.

Weight loss surgery is considered successful when 50 percent of excess weight is removed and the loss is maintained for at least five years. A 100-pound overweight patient, for example, should lose at least 50 pounds; a 200-pound overweight patient should lose at least 100 pounds. They should be able to maintain their weight loss for the next five years.

In the first 1-2 years after a Roux-en-Y gastric bypass, weight loss is estimated to be half to two-thirds of excess weight. This usually equates to 1-2 pounds every week until a new baseline weight is established. Compliance with dietary and physical activity requirements influences final weight. Weight loss of 50% or more has been recorded ten years and longer after gastric bypass surgery. Furthermore, obesity-related comorbidities or disorders improve significantly. This includes a cure rate of more than 80% for diabetes and a cure rate of more than 90% for sleep apnea.

CHAPTER 1: GASTRIC BYPASS SURGERY

Gastric bypass surgery improves the way food is processed in your stomach and small intestine, helping you to lose weight.

After the procedure, you will have a smaller stomach. You won't be hungry if you eat less.

Some regions of your stomach and small intestine, where food is absorbed, will no longer receive food when you eat. Your body will not get all the calories it needs from meals if this happens.

Gastric Bypass Guide
Benefits

The common bariatric surgery is gastric bypass, which has been around for a long time. A gastric sleeve procedure has rapidly gained popularity since 2011 and is now the most popular bariatric surgery procedure (largely the result of Lap Bands losing market share). However, the benefits of gastric bypass surgery should not be diminished as a result of this. It's still the 'gold standard,' in terms of bariatric surgery, for many people. This is the reason:

You're going to slim down. You should expect to lose 70% of your excess weight in the first 18 months after surgery.

After 18 months, this research showed a decrease of 77.5percent of the excess weight.

You will not be able to eat big meals because of the size restriction on your pouches and stomach.

Eating an excessive amount of sugar or carbohydrates will make you unwell (dumping syndrome).

You will consume fewer calories as a result of this (bypassed intestines).

Type 2 diabetes will be reduced or eliminated as a result of your efforts.

You may be able to get rid of your prescriptions for blood pressure and/or cholesterol medications.

Significant weight loss increased testosterone, and an improved metabolism may cause your hormones to alter. According to most studies, 90% of patients retain at least 50percent of their excess weight loss after surgery.

Losing weight and reducing medication make exercising more manageable. It's possible to shed more weight than the above average if you're able to combine regular exercise with a nutritious diet.

After gastric bypass surgery, many people report feeling more energized, more confident, and generally happier. These advantages are difficult to quantify, but a study found that 95% of patients felt better about themselves a year following surgery.

WHY IT'S DONE

Gastric bypass surgery is used to assist you in losing excess weight and lowering your risk of developing potentially fatal weight-related health problems, such as:

- Gastroesophageal reflux disease
- Heart disease
- High blood pressure
- High cholesterol
- Obstructive sleep apnea
- Type 2 diabetes
- Stroke
- Cancer
- Infertility

Typically, gastric bypass is performed only after you have attempted to reduce weight through diet and exercise improvement.

WHO IT'S FOR

In general, if you meet the following criteria, gastric bypass and other weight-loss surgeries may be an option for you:

- Your body mass index (BMI) is equal to or more than 40.
- You have a body mass index (BMI) of 35 to 39.9 (obesity) and a serious weight-related health problem, such as type two diabetes, hypertension, or severe sleep apnea. If your BMI is between 30 and 34 and you have serious weight-related health issues, you may be eligible for some types of weight-loss surgery.

However, gastric bypass is not appropriate for everyone who is morbidly obese. You may need to meet certain medical criteria to be considered for weight-loss surgery. You will very certainly face a rigorous screening process to determine your eligibility.

Additionally, you must be willing to make long-term adjustments in order to live a better lifestyle. You may be expected to participate in long-term follow-up plans that examine your nutrition, lifestyle and behavior, as well as your medical issues.

Consult your health insurance provider or local Medicare or Medicaid office to determine whether your policy covers weight-loss surgery.

HOW DO YOU PREPARE?

In the weeks leading up to your operation, you may be asked to start an exercise plan and refrain from smoking.

Prior to beginning your therapy, you may be limited in what you can eat and drink, as well as which drugs you can take.

WHERE CAN YOU EXPECT IT?

Gastric bypass surgery is carried out in a hospital. Your hospital stay will typically last one to two days, but could continue longer depending on your condition.

WHILE THE PROCEDURE IS RUNNING

You will be given general anesthesia prior to the start of the surgery. Anesthesia is a drug that causes sleep and gives comfort during surgery.

Your individual circumstances and the doctor's practices will define the specifics of your gastric bypass treatment. Certain treatments are carried out through large (open) incisions in the abdomen. The majority, however, are done laparoscopically, which involves inserting equipment through a succession of small abdominal incisions.

Following the open or laparoscopic incisions, the surgeon makes a cut across the top of your stomach, separating it from the rest of your stomach. The resulting pouch is around the size of a walnut and can store about 1 ounce of food. Under normal circumstances, your stomach can hold about three pints of food.

Following that, the surgeon divides the small intestine in half and sews a segment of it directly to the pouch. Following that, food is introduced into this small pouch of the stomach and directly into the associated small intestine. Food bypasses the majority of your stomach and the first segment of your small intestine by going directly through the majority of your stomach and the first section of your small intestine.

Surgery usually takes a few hours. Following surgery, you awaken in a recovery room where medical personnel examine you for any problems.

IMMEDIATELY AFTER THE PROCEDURE

You may consume liquids but not solid foods shortly after gastric bypass surgery to allow your stomach and intestines to heal. Following that, you'll adhere to a personalized nutrition plan that gradually moves you from liquids to pureed foods. After that, you can start with soft things and work your way up to firmer foods as your body tolerates them.

You may be subject to a variety of restrictions or limitations on the amount and type of food and drink that you can consume. Following surgery, your doctor may advise you to take vitamin and mineral supplements, such as a multivitamin containing iron, calcium, and vitamin B-12.

In addition, you'll have regular medical exams for the first several months after weight-loss surgery to check your health. You may need laboratory testing, blood work, and other tests.

CHAPTER 2 : STAGE 1: DIET AND TIPS

1. FAT-FREE CHICKEN BROTH

- Prep Time: 2 hours
- Cook Time: 10 minutes
- Total Time: 2 hours 10 minutes
- Serves: 1

Ingredients

- 1 Whole Chicken
- Salt as need
- Onion as need
- Garlic as need
- Spices of your choice

Instructions

1. Boil all the ingredients in a large saucepan.
2. For a couple of hours, place in refrigerator.
3. When cool, remove from the fridge and then turn off the fat.

Nutrition

Fat and protein make up 142g of the total calories, while fat and sodium account for 112g.

2. LOW-FAT VEGETABLE BROTH

- Prep:20min
- Cook:20min
- Ready in:40min
- Serves: 2

Ingredients

- 120g celery, chopped
- 60g carrots, chopped
- 80g onion, chopped
- 150g green beans, cut
- 1/2 tsp dried basil
- 1/2 tsp dried sage
- 1/2 tsp dried thyme

- 1/2 tsp garlic granules
- 4 cubes chicken stock
- 1.5 liters water

Instructions:

1. A large stockpot of water and some stock cubes should be brought to a rolling boil.
2. Garlic salt and pepper as need. Add the celery and carrots.
3. Bring to a boil again and simmer for 15 minutes or until the veggies are fork-tender.

3. KETO SUGAR-FREE RASPBERRY JELLO CUPS

- Yield: 4 servings
- Prep Time: 8 minutes
- Total Time: 8 minutes

Ingredients

- 1 cup boiling water (3 minutes in the microwave)
- 1 cup cold water
- 3 packets unflavored gelatin
- 1/2 cup monk fruit sweetener
- 3/4 tsp raspberry flavoring (I like this one!)
- 1/2 tsp red food coloring (optional)
- 1/2 cup raspberries
- sugar-free whipped cream for topping (optional)

Instructions

1. In a large bowl, mix the hot water and the monk fruit sweetener (optional). Stir in the sweetener until all of it has dissolved.
2. In a little mixing bowl, combine the cold water and gelatin powder. Allow for a minimum of two minutes of sitting.
3. Whisk for one to two minutes until all ingredients are dissolved after adding the gelatin water to the hot water.
4. Placed the raspberries in the bottom of four dessert cups, dividing them evenly. Do this in four equal portions, and then top with the raspberries.
5. Refrigerate for at least two hours or three days. Sprinkle with extra raspberries and sugar-free whipped cream, if desired, before serving and enjoying!

SATGE 2: FULL LIQUIDS / PUREED FOODS RECIPES & TIPS.

1. ORANGE CREAMSICLE PROTEIN SMOOTHIE

- Prep Time 5 minutes
- Total Time 5 minutes
- Yield: 1

Ingredients

- 1/2 cup orange juice
- 1/2 cup almond milk
- 1/4 cup greek yogurt
- 1 scoop vanilla protein powder
- 1/4 banana
- 1/2 cup ice

Instructions

1. Blend in a large bowl until all ingredients are well mixed.
2. 30 seconds on high-speed blending
3. Enjoy your beverage after it has been poured into a cup.

Nutrition Information:

- Calories in one serving: 245
- Fatty Acids: 2 grams
- 37 grams of carbs
- 22 grams of protein

2. LOW CARB GREEN SMOOTHIE

- Servings: 2 People
- Prep Time: 5 minutes
- Cook Time: 0 minutes
- Total Time: 5 minutes

Ingredients

- 1 medium avocado - peeled and pitted
- 1 cup spinach
- 1 1/2 cups coconut milk, unsweetened
- 1 scoop of sugar-free vanilla protein powder - I recommend this one (It's my favorite and tastes good)

- 1 tbsp peanut butter powder - I love and recommend this one from Naked.
- 1 tbsp freshly squeezed lemon juice

Instructions

1. Blend for 30 seconds with all the ingredients in a blender.
2. Serve immediately after adjusting the flavor with a taste.

Nutrition

- Half a serving has about 168 calories
- 6 grams of carbohydrate,
- 1 gram of polyunsaturated fatty acid,
- 8 grams of monounsaturated fatty acid,
- 1 mg of cholesterol,
- 84 mg of sodium,
- 480 mg of potassium,
- 7 grams of fiber,
- and a single gram of sugar.

3. MANGO PEVERY SMOOTHIE

- Prep Time: 5 mins
- Total Time: 5 mins
- Yield: 2 servings

Ingredients

- 1 ½ cups of almond milk
- 1 cup diced every, fresh or frozen
- 1 cup chopped mango, fresh or frozen
- ½ tsp vanilla extract
- 1 cup ice

Instructions

1. Blend almond milk, every, mango, and vanilla in a food processor or blender until smooth. Make a thorough mix.
2. Blend in the ice until it dissolves completely. If the mixture is too thin, add additional almond milk.

Nutrition

- Calories in one serving: 115
- 18.1 grams of sugar
- 140.4 milligrams of sodium.
- 22.3 grams of carbohydrates

4. PINEAPPLE COCONUT SMOOTHIE

- Prep Time 10 mins
- Total Time 10 mins
- Cuisine American
- Servings 2

Ingredients

- 2 cups of chopped fresh pineapple
- 1/2 cup coconut milk
- 6 oz Greek vanilla or coconut yogurt
- 2 tbsp coconut
- 1 cup ice
- Toasted coconut, for garnish, optional

Instructions

Then, combine everything with the pineapple, coconut milk, yogurt, and coconut flakes in a blender. In a blender, puree the ingredients until completely smooth. In a blender, combine all ingredients and blend until smooth. If using, pour into two glasses and top with toasted coconut. Prepare the dish and serve it as soon as possible.

Nutrition

Per Serving:

- 280 kcal;
- 35 grams carbohydrate;
- 9 grams protein;
- 14 grams fat;
- 27 grams sugar;

5. WATERMELON STRAWBERRY PROTEIN SMOOTHIE

- Prep Time: 10 minutes
- Total Time: 10 minutes
- Servings: 2 smoothies

Ingredients

- 4 cups of chopped watermelon seedless preferred
- 1 cup frozen strawberries
- ¾ cup plant-based yogurt I used Forager project cashew yogurt
- 1-2 Tbsp hemp seeds optional for added protein

Instructions

1. Prepare the watermelon by chopping it up first. Next, place the watermelon chunks, frozen strawberries, vegan yogurt, and hemp seeds in a food processor and process until smooth.
2. In a blender, puree the ingredients until completely smooth. After that, simply pour the contents of two glasses into two glasses and begin drinking immediately!

Nutrition

Per Serving:

- 214 calories,
- 37 grams of carbohydrates,
- 7 grams of protein,
- 6 grams of fat,
- 27 grams of sugar.

6. ROOT VEGETABLE SOUP

- preparation time
- less than 30 mins
- Cooking time
- 30 mins to 1 hour
- Serves 4

Ingredients

- 2 tbsp oil (any type)

- 2 onions, roughly chopped
- 800g/1lb 12oz root vegetables, any kind ,peeled and cut into roughly 2cm/¾in chunks
- 2 garlic cloves, thinly sliced
- 2 chicken or vegetable stock cubes
- ground black pepper
- freshly chopped parsley, to serve (optional)

Method

1. In a large nonstick saucepan, preheat the oil and gently sauté the onions for 6–8 minutes, often turning until tender and beginning to brown.
2. Cook for an additional 5 minutes, occasionally stirring, after adding the vegetable chunks. Cook for another few seconds after adding the garlic.
3. Add the stock cubes and bring to a boil, then reduce the heat and simmer for 20 minutes. Simmer for about twenty minutes, occasionally stirring, until the vegetables are very soft. Reduce the heat to a simmer. Cover loosely with a lid.
4. The pan should no longer be on the stovetop.
5. Use a stick blender to puree the soup until it's smooth and flavorful, then season as needed with salt and pepper. A little hot water can thin down a soup.
6. If desired, serve with the bread after ladling the soup into bowls and garnishing with freshly chopped parsley.

7. GARLIC AND VEGETABLE SOUP

- prep: 20 mins
- cook:1 hr 15 mins
- total:1 hr 35 mins
- Yield: 6 servings

Ingredients

- 2 tbsp olive oil
- 2 carrots, chopped
- 2 stalks celery, chopped
- ¼ medium head cabbage, shredded
- 6 cups of chicken broth
- 2 (14.5 ounces) cans peeled and diced tomatoes
- 3 ½ cups of water

- 1 cup elbow macaroni
- 3 cloves garlic, minced
- ½ tsp ground black pepper

Instructions

1. Medium heat is ideal for heating the oil. Cook the carrots, celery, and cabbage in the oil, frequently stirring, for about 8 minutes.
2. Placed the broth, tomatoes, and water in a large pot and brought to a boil. Boil for 1 hour on low, then remove the lid and simmer for 1 hour more.
3. Trying to remove the lid and stirring in the macaroni will take about 5 minutes. Garlic and freshly ground black pepper should be added after the sauce has been separated from the heat source.

8. CHICKEN CLEAR SOUP

- Total Time 30m
- Prep Time 10 m
- Yield: 3 servings

Ingredients

- 2 cup chicken
- 2 spring onions
- salt as required
- 1 tbsp butter
- 2 egg
- powdered black pepper as required
- water as required

How to make Clear Chicken Soup

1. To begin, prepare a big pot of soup over medium heat. Put the butter in the pan and heat it until it is melted.
2. Add the spring onions to the pan after they have been finely chopped. Cook them for a few minutes until they start to turn golden brown.
3. Toss in the chicken pieces with the butter and spring onions, and cook until the chicken is no longer pink in the middle.

4. Meanwhile, heat water in a large, heavy pot over high heat. Bring a pot of water to a boil, add the meat, and cook until it is tender and the juices have been released into the soup.
5. After the soup has been cooked, strain it into a large bowl or pan and skim off the fat. Let the soup cool, and then test it once more.
6. Reheat the pan on medium heat and then add the soup. Agree to the mixture to boil for a few minutes. In a bowl, beat the egg whites until stiff peaks form. As you continue to stir the soup, slowly add the egg whites in a thin stream.
7. Cook for an additional 2 minutes after adding salt and black pepper seasonings to the soup mixture.
8. Strain the soup one more time and serve it hot in bowls with a garnish of any green herb once it's ready to eat.

9. FLUFFY EGG WHITE OMELETTE

- Prep Time 10 mins
- Cook Time 10 mins
- Total Time 20 mins
- Yield: 1 serving

INGREDIENTS

- 4 large egg whites
- ¼ tsp Diamond Crystal kosher salt
- ⅛ tsp freshly ground black pepper
- ⅛ tsp garlic powder
- 1 tbsp grated Parmesan cheese
- ¼ cup chopped scallions, green parts
- ⅓ cup firm cherry tomatoes halved
- Olive oil spray

INSTRUCTIONS

1. To prepare the dish, heat a nonstick 8-inch skillet for 2-3 minutes on medium heat.
2. Whip the egg whites, salt, pepper, and garlic powder in a medium bowl until frothy. Add the parmesan and mix well.
3. Fold in the green onions and tomatoes with a spatula after the egg whites have been whisked to stiff peaks. Serve immediately. As demonstrated in the video, you can scatter the vegetables on top after pouring the eggs into the skillet. However, I favor whisking them into the eggs before adding them to the skillet.

4. Spray the skillet lightly with olive oil spray, then add the egg whites and cook them while tilting the skillet to ensure that they are spread out evenly throughout the skillet.
5. Reduce the heat to medium-low after a few minutes. The egg whites will cook more quickly if you gently lift the edges of the omelet and tilt the skillet as you go along. This will help the omelet cook more quickly. Carefully flip the omelet when the bottom is cooked, and the top is no longer runny but still wet. When I'm doing meals, I'll use two large spatulas. Use a large plate on top of your skillet (be careful, it will be hot), invert the omelet into the container
6. Assemble the omelet by folding it in thirds and serving on a plate.

10. PROTEIN CHAI LATTE WITH COCONUT MILK FROTH

- Prep Time 10 minutes
- Total Time 10 minutes
- Servings: 1

Ingredients

- 10-12 oz brewed chai tea
- 1 scoop Cellucor Cinnamon Swirl Whey Protein
- 2 tbsp light coconut milk
- 45 mg pure Stevia or 1 packet sweetener of choice

Instructions

1. Blend the chai tea with the whey protein in a blender bottle until smooth and mixed. Make a good shake before using (opening the lid to release pressure as needed until soft).
2. Pour the remaining chai mix into a mug and set aside 2 tbsp for serving. Shake the reserved chai mixture well before adding the coconut milk and Stevia.
3. To help keep the protein chai atop the coconut milk foam, place a spoonful on top of the mixture. If you'd like, top with cinnamon powder.

11. CHOCOLATE PROTEIN SHAKE

- Prep Time 10 minutes
- Total Time 10 minutes
- Servings 1 large

Ingredients

- 3/4 cup unsweetened vanilla almond milk
- 1 scoop (1/4 cup + 1 tbsp (32g)) good-quality chocolate protein powder
- 1 tbsp Dutch-process cocoa powder
- 1/2 cup frozen banana
- 1 tbsp almond butter or peanut butter
- 1/4 tsp vanilla extract, optional
- 8 ice cubes
- Optional: sweetener as needed

Instructions

IN ADVANCE:

Bananas should be peeled, sliced into large coins, and then frozen in a plastic bag.

BLEND:

Use a powerful blender to mix all of the ingredients. Blend until the mixture is smooth and well-mixed. Re-blend after re-stirring if necessary. In the absence of a powerful blender, an additional 1/4 cup milk may be required.

ENJOY: Enjoy your beverage after it has been poured into a cup.

Recipe Notes

Note 1: When bananas are ripe, slice them into coins and store them in a ziplock bag. Frozen food can be softened in the refrigerator overnight or over several hours.

Note 2: To get the best results, experiment with several protein powders and see what works best for you. Occasionally, I'll add a few drops of Stevia, maple syrup, or honey to my drink. Add to the individual's taste.

12. EASY EGG CUSTARD

- prep:10 mins
- cook:1 hr
- total:1 hr 10 mins
- Yield:6 servings

Ingredients

- 2 cups of milk
- 2 eggs, beaten
- ½ cup white sugar
- 1 pinch salt
- 1 dash vanilla extract
- 1 pinch ground nutmeg (optional)

Instructions

1. Set the oven to 325°F (165 degrees C).
2. In a large bowl, whisk together milk, eggs, sugar, salt, and vanilla until well mixed. Sprinkle nutmeg over the tops of the egg mixture before dividing it among the six custard cups. Prepare custard cups, place them in a baking pan, and add hot water to cover them halfway up the sides.
3. Bake for 1 hr at 350°F or until custards is set. Allow plenty of cooling time.

13. CREAMY HEALTHY SOUP

- Prep: 10 mins
- Cook: 20 mins
- Total: 30 mins
- Servings:5

Ingredients
Healthy Creamy Soup Broth:

- 4 large zucchinis (700g/1.2 lb), peeled and cut into 1.5cm/3/5" slices
- coarsely sliced 1/2 of a large onion (brown, white, yellow)
- 2 garlic cloves, whole
- 2 cups of(500 ml) chicken broth (or veg broth)
- 2 cups of(500 ml) water

- 1/2 tsp every garlic and onion powder (or 1 tsp of one of them)
- 1/4 tsp black pepper
- 1 cup (250 ml) 0% fat milk (or other milk of choice)

Soup Add-Ins:

- 1 tbsp (15g) butter or olive oil
- 2 garlic cloves, minced
- 1/2 large onion, finely chopped
- 1.5 cups of carrot, peeled and finely diced
- 1.5 cups of celery, finely chopped
- 1 small red capsicum/bell pepper, finely chopped
- 1 and a half cups chopped cooked chicken breast
- 3/4 cup frozen peas

Garnish:

- Fresh thyme

Instructions
Healthy Creamy Broth:

Cover the pot with all of the Broth components EXCEPT milk, and bring to a vigorous simmer over medium-high heat.

Decrement the heat to low and simmer for 15 minutes, or until the zucchini is very soft.

Detach the pan from the heat and add the milk to it. Using a handheld blender, blend until smooth. Salt to taste and adjust as needed. The velvety, low-calorie broth will astonish you!

Healthy Cream of Chicken Soup:

Melt the butter in the large pot or saucepan over medium heat.

Toss in the following ingredients: garlic, onion, carrot, and celery. Add the capsicum after cooking for three minutes. Continue to cook for an extra 2 minutes, or until the onion is soft and translucent.

Add the chicken, broth, and peas to the pot and stir to mix. Cook peas for 2 to 3 minutes at a low simmer, stirring occasionally.

Salt and pepper should be adjusted based on the taste.

Pour into bowls and top with a sprinkling of thyme leaves, if desired. Slurp it up and be amazed at how few calories there are in a bowl. This is creamy and delicious!!

Recipe Notes:

1. Storage - broth will easily keep 4 to 5 days in the fridge. It might look split but once heated, stir vigorously, and it will come together. It can also freeze, thaw then reheat.

The same also applies if you make the cream of chicken soup!

Nutrition for Healthy Cream of Chicken Soup (with all the add-ons, that is). The serving size is about 2 and a half cups (enough for a meal). Skip the chicken and peas (high in carbs) and replace them with more celery and carrot for fewer calories.

14. PUMPKIN CARROT SOUP

- Prep Time: 15 minutes
- Cook Time: 35 minutes
- Total Time: 50 minutes
- Yield: 6 servings

Ingredients

- 3 tbsp olive oil
- 1 medium onion, chopped
- 3 cloves of garlic, minced or pressed
- 1 cup pumpkin, chopped into 1-inch pieces
- 1 medium parsley root, chopped
- 3 medium carrots, chopped
- 2 and ½ cups of vegetable stock
- 1 tsp Herbes de Provence spice mix
- ½ cup half and half cream + 2 tbsp for garnish
- salt and pepper, as need
- pinch of chili powder, as need
- fresh herbs and roasted sunflower seeds for garnish (optional)

Instructions

1. In a little saucepan, warm the olive oil over medium heat. For 2 to 3 minutes, add the onion and garlic and cook, occasionally stirring, until translucent—Cook the pumpkin, parsley root, and carrot for an additional 5 minutes, stirring frequently.
2. Stir in the vegetable stock and Herbes de Provence spice blend. Simmer for 25 minutes on low heat with a lid on.

3. Turn off the heat and remove the soup from the stove. Pulse until smooth with an immersion blender or food processor.
4. Simmer for about fifteen minutes, occasionally stirring, until the cream has thickened. Add a dash of hot sauce powder as needed
5. Divide amongst 6 bowls and garnish with a cream swirl, fresh herbs, and sunflower seeds. Serve immediately.

15. PUREED CLASSIC EGG SALAD

- Prep Time 5 mins
- Total Time 5 mins
- Servings: 2

Ingredients

- 2 hard-boiled eggs
- 1 tbsp reduced-fat mayonnaise
- 1 tbsp plain Greek-style yogurt
- Salt and pepper as needed

Instructions

1. 2 boiled eggs, sliced
2. Add the egg slices to a food processor and process until smooth.
3. Chop the eggs until no large pieces remain.
4. Eggs, mayo, Greek yogurt, and seasonings go into a large bowl and are mixed.
5. Blend the egg salad until it's smooth.

Nutrition

A quarter cup of this recipe has 176 calories, 4 grams of carbohydrate, 9 grams of protein, 13 grams of fat, 4 grams of saturated fat, 7 grams of polyunsaturated fat, and no trans fat. It also has 200.4 milligrams of cholesterol, 144.9 milligrams of sodium, and 4 grams of fiber.

16. BLUEBERRY LEMONADE VITAMIN SMOOTHIE

- Prep Time: 5 minutes
- Cook Time: 0 minutes
- Total Time: 5 minutes
- Servings: 1

Ingredients

- 1 - 2 scoops of protein powder
- 1/2 cup canned full-fat coconut milk (plain or vanilla almond milk) 1/2 cup unsweetened
- 1/2 cup ice cubes
- 1 cup blueberries (fresh or frozen)
- 1/2 cup baby spinach leaves (optional)
- 1 banana
- 1 tbsp ground flaxseed or chia seeds
- zest from 1 lemon
- 1 tbsp freshly squeezed lemon juice

Instructions

1. Blend all of the ingredients until smooth. Process till everything is nice and smooth. If necessary, add a thimbleful of water to achieve the appropriate consistency. Prepare the food and serve it right away.

Notes

Optional Add-ins:

- 1/2 ripe avocado
- 1 Tbsp unsweetened coconut flakes
- 1 scoop of Green SuperFood or Reds powder
- 1 Tbsp chia seeds
- 1 Tbsp flaxseed Oil
- 1 Tbsp Hempseed

17. STRAWBERRY GREEK YOGURT WHIP

- Prep Time: 10 minutes
- Total Time: 10 minutes
- Servings: 6 servings

Ingredients

- 3 frozen strawberries
- 2/3 cup plain 0% fat Greek yogurt
- 1 tbsp natural no-calorie sweetener
- 1/2 cup light whipped topping

Instructions

1. I am using a small microwave-safe bowl, thaw frozen strawberries. 60 seconds of defrosting time are required.
2. The strawberries in the bowl should be diced with kitchen shears until well-chopped but still a little runny. Stir in the Greek yogurt if using.
3. The sweetener can be added by stirring in a small amount at a time Fold in the light whipped topping before serving. Cover and chill until ready to do, or serve immediately from the refrigerator. It can be eaten on its own or as a dip for yogurt.

Nutrition

calories are 24 kcal.

- There are 3 grams of carbohydrates,
- 2 grams of protein,
- and 1 gram of fat,
- 2 grams of sugar.

18. EGGNOG PROTEIN SHAKE

- Prep Time: 5 mins
- Total Time: 5 mins
- Servings:
- 2 serving

Ingredients

- 1 cup cashew milk
- ¼ cup egg white protein powder
- 1 small frozen banana sliced
- 1 tsp pumpkin pie spice
- 1 tsp vanilla extract
- vanilla stevia or honey as need
- fresh ground nutmeg as need
- ice optional

Instructions

1. Use a high-powered blender to mix the cashew milk, egg white powder, and bananas, as well as the pumpkin pie spice, vanilla, honey, and nutmeg.
2. Grate some nutmeg over the top as a garnish.

Nutrition

- Calories in one serving: 187
- 17 grams of carbs
- 24g of protein
- 1 gram of fat
- 9 grams of sugar

19. CREAMY CARROT AND GINGER SOUP

- Prep Time 5 minutes
- Cook Time 30 minutes
- Total Time 35 minutes
- Servings 5

Ingredients

- 1 tbsp coconut oil
- 1 chopped medium yellow onion
- 1 clove garlic minced
- 3 tbsp chopped fresh ginger*
- 1 pound chopped and peeled carrots (baby carrots are also fine)
- 24-32 oz vegetable broth**
- 1 14 oz can of coconut cream or coconut milk
- 1/2 tsp salt + more as needed

Instructions

For the Stovetop:

1. Prepare a big skillet for cooking by heating it to medium-high heat. Melt the coconut oil in a bit of saucepan over low heat.
2. Cook for about 5 minutes, or until the onion is soft and translucent, after which add the onion, garlic, and ginger.
3. Bring to a boil the carrots, vegetable broth, and stock.
4. Simmer the pot at a low temperature—Cook for 25 minutes, or until carrots are very soft. Add the coconut milk and whisk until mixed (or coconut cream if using).
5. Blend the soup until it's smooth using an immersion blender. Alternatively, you can blend in batches with a conventional blender. Taste for salt and adjust as necessary. Serve immediately.

For the Instant Pot:

1. Use your IP's saute feature to prepare the food. When the mixture is heated, add the onion and the oil—Stir-fry for a further 2 minutes, after which you can add the garlic and ginger.
2. On your IP, click the Cancel button to end the session. Add 3 cups of (24 ounces) of broth and the carrots. Put the cover on tightly. Once you've done that, pick the manual setting and cook for 6 minutes at high pressure.
3. Consider using a quick-release cable. Mix in the salt and coconut milk thoroughly (add more as needed if needed).
4. Blend until smooth, either with a regular blender or with an immersion blender.

5. Serve immediately.

20. CLASSIC TOMATO SOUP

- Prep Time: 15 minutes
- Cook Time: 40 minutes
- Total Time: 55 minutes
- Yield: 4 bowls

Ingredients

- 2 tbsp extra-virgin olive oil
- 1 medium yellow onion, chopped
- ½ tsp acceptable sea salt
- 2 tbsp tomato paste
- 1 large can (28 ounces) of whole tomatoes, with their liquid
- 2 cups of vegetable broth
- ½ cup washed and drained Great Northern or Cannellini beans
- 2 tbsp unsalted butter, cut into a few pieces
- 1 tsp coconut sugar or brown sugar, as need
- Freshly ground black pepper, as need
- For the tomato-basil variation (optional): ten to fifteen fresh basil leaves, as need

Instructions

1. Warm the olive oil to a shimmering state in a Dutch oven or soup pot over medium heat. Cook, stirring periodically, for 7 to 10 minutes, until the onions are soft and transparent. Cook the tomato paste for 30 seconds, stirring regularly until it begins to smell good.
2. Be sure to mix the tomatoes with the vegetable broth once you add them. Make a simmer by increasing the heat to medium-high and adding the mixture. It should be ready in about thirty minutes, with heat reduced to a low simmer and occasionally stirring to ensure it stays hot.
3. After taking it off the heat, let it cool for a few minutes. Transfer the mixture with care to a blender, being careful not to overfill it over the line where the blender will accept it (blend in batches if necessary). Add the beans, butter, sugar, and a generous amount of freshly ground black pepper to the pot and stir to mix. Blend the soup until smooth, taking care not to allow any hot steam to escape through the cover.

4. To compensate for the varying flavors of canned tomatoes, I usually have to adjust to the recipe before serving. In case extra sugar (to counteract the acidity of the tomatoes), pepper, or salt is needed (I usually add another 1/4 to 1/2 tsp), taste and adjust as desired.
5. If you're going to include basil, do it right away. Serve immediately after a final blend. This soup will keep for approximately four days in the refrigerator. Leftovers will keep for up to three months in the freezer.

21. MEXICAN EGG PUREE

- Yields 8 Servings
- Prep Time 13 mins
- Cook Time 13 mins
- Total Time 26 mins

Ingredients

- ½ lb Loose turkey sausage
- 6 Eggs
- 1 tbsp Full fat plain Greek yogurt
- 1 tsp Cumin
- ½ tsp Paprika
- ¼ cup dried and rinsed black beans with no salt added
- 2 tbsp Cilantro, chopped

Instructions

1. Whisk the eggs, Greek yogurt, cumin, and paprika together until well mixed in a large mixing bowl. Stir in the other ingredients. Place on the back burner.
2. Saute the turkey sausage in a bit of oil in a large skillet over medium heat. Cook for 5-6 minutes until thoroughly cooked while stirring to break up any clumps.
3. Reduce the temperature to a low-medium setting. To stir the egg mixture for 2-3 minutes, use a rubber spatula.
4. To reheat the black beans, add them to the pot and cook for 1 minute. Include chopped cilantro in the mix.
5. Add cilantro and 2 tbsp of water to a food processor or blender. Using a food processor, pulse the ingredients until well mixed.

22. CHIMICHURRI CHICKEN PUREE

- Yields 5 Servings
- Prep Time 13 mins
- Cook Time 13 mins
- Total Time 26 mins

Ingredients

- ½ lb Lean ground chicken
- ½ tsp Paprika
- ¼ tsp Dried oregano
- ¼ cup Parsley
- 2 tbsp Cilantro
- 2 cloves garlic, peeled
- 2 tsp Apple cider vinegar

Instructions

1. 2 tbsp water in a saute pan on medium-high heat Chicken, paprika, and oregano should all be added simultaneously to the pan. Cook for 6-8 minutes, breaking up the pieces as they cook until the meat is tender. To prevent the pan from drying out, add 1 Tbsp of water at a time as the liquid evaporates.
2. Garlic, apple cider vinegar, and 3 tbsp of water should be mixed in a food processor or blender. Pulse the contents in a food processor until very finely minced.
3. Stir in the chimichurri until it is well-coated.
4. Process until smooth by returning to food processor and processing till.

23. GROUND TURKEY BURRITOS WITH REFRIED BEANS

- Prep: 15 mins
- Cook: 30 mins
- Total: 45 mins
- Servings: 12 servings

Ingredients

- 2 tbsp vegetable oil
- 2 pounds ground turkey breast
- 1 cup onion, chopped
- 2 cloves garlic, finely minced
- 1 (15-ounce) can refried beans
- 1/2 cup salsa
- 2 (4-ounce) cans every mild and green chile peppers, chopped
- 1 or 2 tbsp finely chopped jalapeño peppers, optional
- 2 tsp chili powder
- 2 tsp ground cumin
- 1 tsp dried oregano
- 10 to 12 (8-inch) flour tortillas
- 1 1/2 cups Mexican blend shredded cheese

Instructions

1. the ingredients must be gathered
2. Pre heat the vegetable oil in a large skillet over medium heat. Sautee the onion and turkey in a skillet until no longer pink.
3. Then add the garlic and all other ingredients, including the beans and salsa (including the jalapenos), and mix well.
4. Stirring constantly, bring to a simmer. For about 20 minutes, cover and stir frequently.
5. Follow the package instructions for heating the tortillas. Melt 2 to 3 tbsp of cheese in a small skillet over medium heat.
6. Add roughly half a cup of the cooked turkey mixture on the top of every serving. Wrap the meat in the tortilla by tucking the ends under and rolling it up. Continue with the rest of the burritos.
7. To serve, top the burritos with salsa and more cheese if desired.

24. CHICKEN AND BLACK BEAN MOLE PUREE

- Yields 8 Servings
- Prep Time 12 mins
- Cook Time 12 mins
- Total Time 24 mins

Ingredients

- 1 Clove of Garlic, Minced
- ½ lb lean ground chicken
- 1 cup no salt added black beans, rinsed and drained
- 3 tbsp raw almonds, soaked in water overnight*
- ¼ cup low sodium chicken broth
- ½ tbsp raw cacao powder
- ½ tsp paprika
- ¼ tsp dried oregano
- ¼ tsp umin
- ¼ tsp coriander
- ¼ tsp garlic powder
- ⅛ tsp cinnamon
- 2 tbsp cilantro, chopped

Instructions

1. 2 tbsp water in a saute pan on medium-high heat. Cook for 1 minute, frequently stirring, until aromatic with garlic.
2. Cook the chicken for 6-8 minutes, breaking it up with a spoon as it cooks until it is thoroughly done. To prevent the pan from drying out, add 1 Tbsp of water at a time as the liquid evaporates.
3. Blend or process 2 tbsp water with the soaked almonds and the rest of the ingredients (including the garlic powder and cinnamon) in a food processor or blender until smooth. Process till everything is nice and smooth.
4. Bring chicken, sauce, and black beans to a boil—mix ingredients in a blender or food processor and process until smooth.
5. Almonds can be soaked quickly by placing them in a small pot with water and covering them completely. Reduce to a low heat and continue simmering for 15-20 minutes, or until the fruit is plump to your preference.

25.   PUMPKIN PIE PROTEIN SHAKE

- Prep Time: 5 minutes
- Cook Time: 10 minutes
- Total Time: 15 minutes
- Servings: 2 People

Ingredients

- 1/2 Cup Canned pumpkin puree
- 1 medium banana sliced and frozen
- 1 cup Vanilla Greek yogurt
- ¼ Tsp pumpkin pie spice
- 1 Scoop Whey Protein vanilla
- ¼ Cup Almond milk
- light whipped cream and pumpkin pie spice are optional garnishes.

Instructions

1. You can use a food processor or a blender to mix all of the ingredients except the banana and protein powder, and almond milk.
2. Blend the ingredients in a blender until they are entirely smooth.
3. Whip cream and pumpkin pie spice can be added to the drink before serving if desired.

Nutrition

This meal has 216 calories, 35 grams of carbohydrates, 15 grams of protein, and 2 grams of fat. It has a Sodium content of 116 milligrams and a Potassium content of 569 milligrams. It has 4 grams of fiber and 23 grams of sugar.

26. GINGERBREAD COOKIE PROTEIN SHAKE

- Prep Time: 3 minutes
- Total Time: 3 minutes
- Servings: 1

Ingredients

- 1 Cup Milk Substitute - or Milk (8 Ounces)
- 1 Tbsp Syrup - Sugar-Free
- ½ Tsp Vanilla Extract
- ¼ Tsp Butter Extract
- 3 Tbsp Liquid Egg Whites - 46g Pasteurized
- 1 Scoop Protein Powder - 30g Vanilla Protein Powder
- ⅛ Tsp Ground Allspice
- ½ Tsp Ground Cinnamon
- ¼ Tsp Ground Ginger
- 1 Packet Sweetener
- ½ Sheet Graham Cracker - Low Fat Cinnamon
- 5.3 Ounces Greek Yogurt - 150g Fat-Free Vanilla
- ½ Cup Ice

Instructions

In a large mixing basin, combine all of the ingredients.

Nutrition

- 322 kcal,
- 29g carbs,
- 38g protein,
- 6g total fat,
- 451 mg sodium,
- 16g sugar

27. LEMON GARLIC PUREED SALMON

- Prep Time 10 mins
- Servings: 3

Ingredients

- 5 ounces canned salmon
- 2 Tbsp Reduced-fat mayonnaise
- 1 tsp lemon juice
- 1/8 tsp garlic powder

Instructions

1. Take the canned salmon from the water and pat dry with a paper towel.
2. Process the salmon in a food processor until smooth and creamy.
3. Add the mayonnaise, garlic, and lemon juice and stir until well-mixed and smooth.
4. Blend the ingredients in a blender until they are entirely smooth.

Notes

- Don't care for canned tuna? If desired, a cooked salmon fillet or tuna can be used.
- You can adjust the amount of lemon and garlic to your preference.

Nutrition

- A 0.25 cup portion
- 88 calories
- 1 gram carbohydrate,
- 11 gram protein,
- 41 mg cholesterol
- 250 mg sodium

28. SINGLE-SERVE BAKED RICOTTA

- Prep Time 5 mins
- Cook Time 20 mins
- Total Time 25 mins
- Servings: 5

Ingredients

- Olive Oil Spray
- 15- ounce Part-skim ricotta
- ⅓ cup parmesan cheese
- ⅛ tsp basil
- ⅛ tsp garlic powder
- Pinch of Salt and pepper
- Optional top with marinara sauce smooth, not chunky

Instructions

1. Pre heat the oven at 350 degrees Fahrenheit before you begin.
2. Place five ramekins on a baking pan and spray with olive oil before serving.
3. Mix the ricotta, parmesan, basil, garlic powder, salt, and pepper in a medium bowl.
4. Mix ricotta and remaining ingredients in a large bowl by stirring well.
5. Fill the prepared ramekins about two-thirds of the way complete with the ricotta mixture.
6. Add a smear of smooth marinara sauce on top.
7. 20 minutes in the oven should suffice.
8. Ideally, serve this dish when it's still warm.

Nutrition

- 144 calories
- 3 grams of carbohydrate
- 12 grams of protein
- 3 grams of fat

29. CREAMY SHRIMP SCAMPI

- Prep: 10 mins
- Cook: 10 mins
- Total: 20 mins
- Serves: 4

Ingredients

- 1 tbsp olive oil
- 1 pound (500 grams) shrimp, tails on or off
- Salt and pepper, as need
- 2 tbsp unsalted butter
- 6 cloves garlic minced
- 1/2 cup unsweetened white wine* or chicken broth
- 1 1/2 cups of reduced-fat cream**
- 1/2 cup fresh grated Parmesan cheese
- 2 tbsp fresh chopped parsley

Instructions

1. Using medium high heat, heat the oil in a large pan. The shrimp should be opaque in the middle and pink on the outside after 1-2 minutes on each side. Toss everything together in a basin and place in the fridge to cool.
2. Melt the butter in the same pan. Cook the garlic in a bit of oil until it starts to smell good (about 30 seconds). Put a little white wine or chicken stock in the pan and cook until it is reduced by half, scraping out any browned parts as you go.
3. Reduce the heat to low-medium, add the cream, and cook, stirring regularly, until the cream is slightly thickened. Taste and combine spices with salt and pepper.
4. Stir in the parmesan cheese and cook for a further minute or two until the cheese has melted and the sauce has thickened somewhat.
5. Re-add the shrimp to the pan and season with salt and pepper as needed. Taste the sauce and make any necessary salt and pepper adjustments based on your findings.
6. Prepare pasta, rice, or steamed vegetables and serve with the sauce on top.

Notes

Use a dry white wine of proper quality, such as chardonnay or pinot grigio.

White wine can be used in place of chicken broth, or it can be omitted out entirely. The sauce will have a different flavor.

For this recipe, I use light (or reduced-fat) cream. If desired, substitute half-and-half, being cautious not to overheat the sauce or it may curdle. As a low-calorie alternative, you can alternatively use evaporated milk

It's also possible to use heavy or thickened cream instead of cornstarch to thicken it. Allow the cream to decrease until it has thickened to your taste over a low heat.

Nutrition

- At 488 calories
- 4 grams of carbohydrates
- 30 grams of protein.
- 44 grams of fat
- 110 milligrams of sodium
- 223 milligrams of potassium.

30. CHOCOLATE PEANUT BUTTER PROTEIN SHAKE

- Prep Time: 5 minutes
- Cook Time: 0 minutes
- Total Time: 5 minutes
- Yield: 1 large smoothie

Ingredients

- 1 large banana, peeled, sliced, and frozen
- 3 Tbsp unsweetened cocoa powder
- 6 oz Chobani 0% Greek yogurt
- 3/4 gallon of skim milk
- 1 Tbsp honey, maple syrup, or agave
- 1 Tbsp peanut butter

Instructions

1. If using a frozen banana, make sure you have a powerful blender to handle the job. Either the Ninja or the Vitamix appeal to me.
2. Blend on high until thick and smooth, adding ingredients one at a time, following the indicated order. To get a more pronounced chocolate flavor, I would begin with 2 Tbsp of cocoa powder. Blend, and then add 1 more. You may need to pause and stir/scrape down the edges of your blender a few times, depending on your blender.
3. If you'd like, you can add 1 tsp of chocolate syrup to the glass before serving.

Notes

This simple smoothie lends itself to endless experimentation. You can skip honey if you want a less sweet smoothie. If you prefer a hotter peanut butter flavor, use more of it. If you'd like a thinner smoothie, just add a little more milk. Increase the nutritional value by including 1 cup of your favorite greens.

31. LOW-FAT REFRIED BEANS

- prep:10 mins
- cook:15 mins
- total:25 mins
- Yield:4 servings

Ingredients

- 2 cups of canned black beans, divided
- ½ cup water
- 2 cloves garlic, minced
- 1 tsp pepper
- 1 tsp salt
- 1 tsp liquid smoke flavoring
- ¾ cup diced onion

Directions

1. 2/3 cup of beans, mashed into a smooth paste in a small bowl.
2. The remaining beans and water should be mixed in a medium-sized pot and heated to a simmer over medium heat. Garlic, pepper, salt, and liquid smoke can be added after the meat has finished cooking.

3. Mix the entire beans with the bean paste and give them a good stir. Add the onion and simmer, stirring occasionally, for 10 minutes, or until softened.

Nutrition Facts

- 130 calories,
- 7.7grams of protein,
- 23.3% of your daily carbohydrate

32. PUMPKIN CURRY SOUP WITH CHICKEN

- Prep Time: 5 minutes
- Cook Time: 20 minutes
- Total Time: 25 minutes
- Servings: 5 servings

Ingredients

- 1 tbsp olive oil
- 1 small onion diced
- 1 red pepper diced
- 2 garlic cloves minced
- 2 cups of no-salt-added chicken broth
- 2 tbsp red curry paste
- 2 cups of pure pumpkin puree can use fresh or canned
- 1 400mL can coconut milk
- 1/2 tsp paprika
- 3 cups of shredded
- 1/2 tsp salt or as need
- Freshly ground pepper as needed
- 1/2 cup loosely packed cilantro chopped

Optional garnishes (but highly recommended):

- Additional cilantro
- Lime juice
- Sliced avocado
- Baked crispy whole-wheat tortilla strips or pita chips*

Instructions

1. Sauté red pepper, onion, and garlic in olive oil for 5 minutes or until nearly tender.
2. Until smooth, mix the next five ingredients. Add the shredded chicken and mix well. Bring to boil, reduce to low heat, and cook for 10 minutes, frequently stirring, until tender. If desired, season with salt and pepper.
3. Add the cilantro right before serving. If desired, top with a squeeze of lime juice, more cilantro, chopped avocado, and crispy baked tortilla or pita chips. Serve immediately with tortilla chips.

Notes

Adding a little additional broth or coconut milk to thin out the soup if it has been sitting for a while may be necessary.

Although the garnishes are listed as "optional" in the recipe, using them is HIGHLY RECOMMENDED for the best taste. One lime juice and half a cup of cilantro flavored the soup. After that, I sprinkled some diced avocado and fresh cilantro over the top of every serving.

This soup tastes best with a crunchy dipping sauce that may be dropped into the soup or used to scrape up the chicken bits. It's easy to make crispy whole-grain or corn tortilla chips by cutting them into wedges or strips and baking them in the oven at 375°F for approximately 10-15 minutes until they're lightly browned and crunchy. Keep an eye on them because they tend to burn quickly.

For meal preparing or batch cooking, this is a terrific recipe. Freeze individual containers or large Ziploc bags of the soup after making a double or triple batch for future meals.

Nutrition

- 296 calories,
- 15 grams of carbohydrate and protein,
- 21 grams of fat,
- 420 milligrams of sodium.

33. ROASTED RED PEPPER & BLACK BEAN ENCHILADAS

- Servings 10
- Prep Time: 20 mins
- Cook Time: 15 mins

Ingredients

- 10 flour tortillas (small to medium-sized)
- 2 red bell peppers, cored and deseeded
- 2 tbsp oil
- 2 14 oz canned black beans, drained
- 1 tsp garlic powder
- 1 cup enchilada sauce
- 3/4 cup Mexican blend cheese
- salt as need

Instructions

1. Broil peppers at the very top of the oven's broiler setting. Brush the oil on the peppers after they've been deseeded and cored. Place carefully on a baking sheet in the oven. Then remove the pan and turn the peppers over. Continue until the peppers are thoroughly cooked and highly charred/roasted, about 3 minutes (10-12 minutes total). Take from heat and allow to cool for a few minutes. Peel the peppers' skin off with care using a paper towel. After that, cut the peppers into dice and set them aside.
2. Add the beans to a pot over low to medium heat and season with salt and garlic powder as needed. Simmer for 8-10 minutes. Add a little bit of stirring every now and again. Reduce and thicken the beans and liquid.
3. Putting together the enchiladas: Pour an even layer of enchilada sauce into your baking dish and spread it out thinly. Then fold up the tortillas and set them in a baking tray with a spoonful of black beans and a sprinkling of sliced peppers. Continue until all of the ingredients have been used. Cover with the remaining sauce and cheese. Top with avocados and chopped cilantro and bake for 15 minutes at 350 degrees Fahrenheit, uncovered. Enjoy!

Notes

For 3-5 days, store leftovers in the fridge in an airtight glass jar. Reheat in a 350F oven covered with foil or in a microwave oven at 50 percent power.

Do not bake frozen enchiladas; instead, assemble them in a dish with sauce and cheese. Freeze for 1-2 months after being well-wrapped with plastic wrap. When you're ready to cook, just take it out of the freezer and let it defrost for the needed amount of time in the oven at 350°F.

Nutrition Facts

- 92% of calories come from fat
- 718.7mg of sodium (30%)
- Carbohydrates: 42.4 grams (14% of total calories)
- Amount of protein 11.8 grams (24%)

34. GREEN PROTEIN SMOOTHIE

- Prep Time 1 min
- Cook Time 5 mins
- Total Time 6 mins
- Servings: 1

Ingredients

- 1 cup unsweetened coconut milk
- 1 banana frozen
- 1 tbsp peanut butter
- 1½ cups of fresh baby spinach lightly packed
- 1 scoop vanilla protein powder
- Ice as needed

Instructions

- All the components, save the unsweetened coconut milk, should be placed in a blender, starting with the coconut milk. Almond or rice milk are also options.
- Blend until smooth and silky. To properly break down all of the spinach leaves, it may take some more time.
- Until the appropriate consistency is achieved, keep adding ice cubes as needed.
- If it becomes too thick, thin it up with a little more coconut milk.

35. WHITE BEAN SOUP

- Prep Time 10 mins
- Cook Time 15 mins
- Total Time 30 mins
- Servings: 6 servings

Ingredients

- 1 tbsp olive oil
- 1 tbsp butter
- 1 thinly sliced yellow onion
- peeled and chopped into coins, one large carrot
- 3 stalks celery, sliced
- 1/4 cup chopped fresh parsley
- 4 cloves garlic, minced
- 6 cups of low sodium vegetable broth or chicken broth
- 1 tsp kosher salt
- 1/2 tsp fresh ground pepper
- 1/2 tsp dried oregano
- 1 bay leaf
- 2 cans (15.5 ounces, every) Great Northern Beans, rinsed and drained
- 1 cup (from a can) corn kernels, rinsed and drained
- 2 cups of fresh baby spinach
- Grated parmesan cheese for serving (optional)
- Toasted bread slices, for serving (optional)

Instructions

1. Melt butter and olive oil in a six-quart Dutch oven or stockpot over medium heat.
2. Pour hot oil over vegetables and simmer for 5 minutes or until they are just starting to thaw.
3. Cook for another 30 seconds, occasionally stirring, after which add the garlic.
4. To that, add the vegetable broth and season with salt, pepper, oregano, and bay leaf, if using. Stir well to mix.
5. Set the heat to a simmer for 5 minutes after the water has boiled.
6. 5 minutes after adding the beans and corn kernels, stir in the kale and boil until tender. Adjust the seasonings according to the taste.
7. One minute after adding the spinach, remove it from the heat.
8. Remove from the heat and let cool.
9. Sprinkle parmesan cheese over soup and serve with toasted bread slices ladled from the pot.

36. CARROT LEMONDE SMOOTHIE

- prep: 15 mins
- cook: 30 mins
- chill: 2 hrs
- total: 2 hrs 45 mins
- Servings: 6

Ingredients

- one pound carrots, peeled and cut into chunks
- 2 cups of water
- 3 cups of pineapple juice and/or unsweetened white grape juice
- ¾ cup lemon juice
- Coldwater
- Ice
- Lemon wedges

Instructions

1. Carrots and water should be mixed in a medium pot. Bring to a boil, then lower the heat to a simmer and cover the pot. Fork-tender vegetables need 30 minutes to cook, stirring occasionally. Blend after the mixture has been allowed to cool slightly. 1 cup of pineapple juice should be added now. Place the cover on the blender and process until smooth.
2. Alternatively, pour into a large pitcher or plastic beverage container to save space on your bar cart. Sum up the rest of the pineapple juice and the lemon juice and mix well. Put the lid on the container and place in the refrigerator for two to twenty-four hours. In order to achieve the appropriate consistency, add 1 to 2 cups of water to the mixture and whisk until smooth.
3. With ice cubes and lemon slices, serve.

Nutrition Facts

- 107 calories per serving
- 27 grams of carbohydrate,
- 3 grams of insoluble fiber,
- 17 grams of sugars,

37. SILKY SWEET POTATO PUREE

- Yield: 8 servings

Ingredients

- 3 pounds whole sweet potatoes, pricked with a fork
- ½ tsp salt and freshly ground pepper, as need
- ½ cup buttermilk
- ½ cup whole milk
- 6 tbsps butter

Instructions

1. Heat the Stove to 425 degrees with the rack in the upper-middle position. Bake the potatoes for 45-60 minutes, or until they are soft when pierced with a fork. When it's safe to handle after the fruit has cooled, peel it.
2. Combine all of the ingredient (except the salt and pepper) in a food processor and process until smooth. While the engine is running, slowly pour in the milk and butter using the feeder tube. Process until silky smooth, perhaps a minute or two. Refrigerate for up to 2 days in an airtight container. Serve the food after it has been warmed through.

38. BUFFALO-RANCH SLOW-COOKER CHICKEN

- Prep 10 min
- Total 4 hr 10 min
- Servings

Ingredients

- one package (28 oz) boneless skinless chicken thighs
- 1 package (1 oz) ranch dressing and seasoning mix
- 1 bottle (12 oz) Buffalo wing sauce

Instructions

1. Toss the chicken with the seasoning mix in a large basin until it is well-coated.
2. Top with Buffalo sauce and place in a 4- to 5-quart slow cooker. Cook the chicken for 4 - 5 hours on low heat, covered until it is fork-tender.

3. Put the chicken in a bowl once you remove it from the slow cooker. Use two forks to shred the chicken. Reintroduce the chicken to the slow cooker sauce, coating it well. Ideally, serve this dish when it's still warm.

Nutrition Information

- A 420-calorie
- 23 grams of total fat,
- 44 grams of protein,
- 8 grams of carbohydrate,
- 2 grams of sugar.

39. CHILI PUREE

- Yield: Makes 3/4 to 1 cup

Ingredients

- 3 ounces dried New Mexico or California chilies (9 to 12; every about 4 in. long)
- ? cup chopped shallots
- ½ tsp ground cinnamon
- Salt and pepper

Instructions

1. Rinse the chilies thoroughly. To get as many seeds out of the plant as possible, cut and discard the stems. Cut the chilies into 1/2-inch pieces with scissors and place them in a 1- to 2-quart baking dish. Add onions, cinnamon, and 1 1/2 cups of water. Cook for 5-10 minutes until the chilies are tender after bringing to a boil over high heat and then reducing heat, covering, and simmering. In a blender, combine each ingredient and blend until totally smooth. Strain the purée into a bowl using a strainer placed over the top of it. Add a pinch of kosher salt and freshly ground black pepper as needed.

Nutrition Facts

- 6 calories per serving,
- 45 percent of which come from fat;
- protein is 2 grams,
- fat is 3 grams,

40. NO CHEW CHEESEBURGERS

- Prep: 20 minutes
- Cook: 10 minutes
- MAKES 4 SERVINGS

Ingredients:

- 8 oz. raw extra-lean ground beef (4% fat or less)
- 1/4 cup finely chopped onion
- 3 tbsp. whole-wheat panko breadcrumbs
- 2 tbsp. egg whites (about 1 large egg's worth) or fat-free liquid egg substitute
- 1/4 tsp. garlic powder
- 1/4 tsp. onion powder
- 1/8 tsp. every salt and black pepper
- 4 slices reduced-fat cheddar cheese
- 16 hamburger dill pickle chips
- 16 small pieces of lettuce
- 8 cherry tomatoes, halved
- Optional dips/toppings: ketchup, yellow mustard, light Thousand Island dressing

Directions:

1. Set the Stove to 400 degrees and prepare the food in it. Use nonstick spray to coat a baking sheet.
2. Combining all ingredients thoroughly in a big bowl will ensure a tender and flavorful finished product.
3. On a baking sheet, evenly divide the mixture into 16 patties—place in oven and bake for 8 mins, or until done to your liking.
4. Meanwhile, cut every slice of cheese into four equal squares.
5. Top burger patties with cheese, pickle chips, lettuce, and tomato halves on a plate as soon as they're done cooking. Serve toothpicks with the meal.

41. ITALIAN CHICKEN PUREE

- Servings: 1 serving

Ingredients

- 1/4 cup canned chicken
- 1 1/2 tbsp tomato sauce
- 1/8 tsp salt
- 1/8 tsp pepper
- 1 tsp Italian seasoning

Instructions

1. Blend all ingredients with a fork or a mini blender until well mixed, and the mixture appears soft.
2. Heat for 30 seconds in a microwave-safe bowl.
3. Alternate option: make lasagne with low-fat cottage cheese or ricotta.

Nutrition

- 106 calories,
- 3 grams of carbohydrate,
- 13 grams of protein,
- 4 grams of fat,
- 1 gram of fiber,
- 1 g of sugar

42. CREAMY RICOTTA AND WHITE BEAN DIP

- Prep: 15 minutes
- Serves: 6

Ingredients:

- 400g can butter beans, drained and rinsed
- 250g tub Perfect Italiano Ricotta
- 1 clove garlic, crushed
- 1 tsp grated lemon rind
- 1 tbsp lemon juice
- 1 tbsp olive oil
- 2 tbsp fresh flat-leaf parsley leaves

- Salt and freshly ground black pepper, as need
- Extra virgin olive oil for drizzling
- Extra parsley leaves for garnish

Instructions

1. Perfect Italiano beans are blended together. Lemon zest and juice in the food processor till smooth. Add in ricotta until well mixed. Add more or less salt if desired.
2. Before serving, pour the dip into a serving dish and let it sit in the fridge for at least an hour.
3. Garnish with parsley and cracked black pepper before serving, and drizzle with extra virgin olive oil

43. GINGER GARLIC TOFU PUREE

- Yields 8 Servings
- Prep Time2 mins
- Cook Time4 mins
- Total Time6 mins

Ingredients:

- 1 tbsp coconut aminos
- 1 tbsp ginger, minced
- 1 clove garlic, minced
- 16 oz firm tofu, cubed

Instructions

1. Coconut aminos, ginger, garlic, and 1/4 cup water are cooked in a skillet over medium-high heat with the ingredients listed above. Bring the mixture to a rolling boil.
2. Cook the tofu for 3-4 minutes until warmed through, stirring periodically. To prevent the pan from drying out, add 1 Tbsp of water at a time as needed.
3. Take from heat and blend in a food processor until smooth.
4. One serving in a small bowl is all you need to eat.

Nutrition Facts
- Calories Per Serving 61.9%
- 3.25 grams of fat is the total.
- Sodium 43mg2 percent
- Saturated Fat.6g3 percent

44. MOROCCAN FISH PUREE

- Yields8 Servings
- Prep Time10 mins
- Cook Time3 mins
- Total Time13 mins

Ingredients:
- One tsp Paprika
- One tsp Cumin
- ¼ tsp Cinnamon
- ¼ tsp Turmeric
- 1 tsp Apple cider vinegar
- 1 Clove garlic, minced
- a white fish fillet weighing eight ounces
- ⅓ cup Light coconut milk
- 1 cup without salt cooked, drained chickpeas, rehydrated
- 2 tbsp Cilantro, chopped

Instructions
1. Paprika, cumin, cinnamon, and turmeric should be heated in a large skillet over medium heat. 1-2 minutes of toasting is sufficient to release the nutty aroma.
2. Garlic, apple cider vinegar, and 2 tbsps of water should be added at this point. Sauté the garlic for 1-2 minutes, or until it begins to smell good.
3. Turn the heat up all the way. Toss up a little fish, coconut milk, and chickpeas for some extra protein. Boil for a couple of mins, then lower the heat to a simmer and cook the fish for 4-6 minutes longer, or until it is done. The thickness of fish affects cooking time. When the fish is cooked correctly, it should be flaky and opaque in color.
4. Remove from the fire and sprinkle with chopped cilantro if using.
5. In a food processor, blend until smooth.

Nutrition Facts

- Calories Per Serving: 66.7% of Daily Value*
- percent of total fat: 1.2 grams
- the percentage of sodium is 33.8 milligrams
- 68% of calories come from carbohydrate sources.
- 1.4 grams of sugars,
- 7.7 grams of protein

45. SESAME TUNA SALAD PUREE

- Yields 8 Servings
- Prep Time5 mins
- Total Time5 mins

Ingredients:

- 1 tbsp Coconut aminos
- 1 tbsp Tahini
- 1 tsp Apple cider vinegar
- 2 tbsp Full fat plain Greek yogurt
- 15 oz Chunk light tuna in water
- 2 tbsp Sesame seeds
- 2 tbsp Parsley, chopped

Instructions

1. Then add the remaining ingredient and stir until well-mixed (about 2 minutes).
2. To mix and break up the tuna, add the sesame seeds and the tuna to the pan. Stir in the parsley until everything is well-mixed.
3. In a food processor, blend until smooth.

Nutrition Facts

- Approximately one-and-a-half ounces per serving
- There are eight servings in every recipe.
- Calories per serving: 78.1% of the RDA *
- 34% of total calories come from fat.
- 9 percent of Sodium: 209,9 milligrams
- Carbohydrate Content: 1.3 grams (1 percent)
- 0.6 grams of sugar.

46. CARIBBEAN PORK PUREE

- Yields 8 Servings
- Prep Time 7 mins
- Cook Time 7 mins
- Total Time 14 mins

Ingredients:

- 1 tsp Garlic powder
- 1 tsp dried thyme
- ½ tsp Dried parsley
- ½ tsp Paprika
- ¼ tsp Allspice
- ¾ lb Lean ground pork
- 1 tbsp Apple cider vinegar
- ¼ cup No salt added black beans
- ¼ cup Cilantro, chopped

Instructions

1. Heat the garlic powder, thyme, parsley, paprika, and allspice in a large skillet until fragrant, about 2-3 mins.
2. Add the meat and 2 tbsp water and raise the heat to high. Blow up while stirring and cook for 5-7 minutes, or until done. To prevent the pan from drying out, add 1 Tbsp water as needed.
3. Add black beans and apple cider vinegar to the pot. Just enough time to warm the beans, about 1-2 minutes. Bring to a boil, then remove from heat and sprinkle with cilantro if using.
4. Process in a food processor until smooth.

47. ROSEMARY CHICKEN WITH BLUE CHEESE

- Yields 8 Servings
- Prep Time 3 mins
- Cook Time 15 mins
- Total Time 18 mins

Ingredients:

- 2 tbsp raw sunflower seeds
- 8 oz lean ground chicken
- 1 clove garlic, minced
- 2 tbsp fresh rosemary, chopped, chopped
- one cup no salt added chickpeas drained and rinsed
- 1 oz reduced-fat blue cheese, crumbled
- 2 tbsp low fat plain Greek yogurt
- 1 tsp apple cider vinegar

Instructions

1. Amass all the ingredients you'll need before you start cooking.
2. Sunflower seeds can be toasted in a skillet over medium heat for 2-3 minutes, turning frequently. Take it out and place it in a different location.
3. Using the same pan, bring 2 tbsps of water to a boil over high heat. Cook for one minute, frequently stirring, until aromatic with garlic. Include chicken in the mix. Cook for 6-8 minutes, breaking up the pieces as they cook until the meat is tender. To prevent the pan from drying out, add 1 Tbsp of water at a time as the liquid evaporates.
4. Stir in the rosemary and chickpeas before serving. To reheat, cook for an additional 1-2 minutes.
5. Apple cider vinegar and blue cheese are mixed in a small basin.
6. Take the chicken out of the heat and set it aside. Then, add the blue cheese cream sauce and mix it all with a wooden spoon. Add roasted sunflower seeds on the top if desired.
7. Process the mixture until it is smooth in a food processor.
8. To enjoy, take one serving and place it in the middle of your plate.

Nutrition Facts

- Total Fat 1.2g 6%
- Sodium 137.3mg 6 percent
- Cholesterol 22.2mg 8%

- Carbohydrate Content: 6.2 grams percent
- .5g of sugars,
- 8.9g of protein, 18%

48. MEDITERRANEAN CHICKEN PUREE

- Yields2 Servings
- Prep Time2 mins
- Cook Time4 mins
- Total Time6 mins

ingredients

- 3 oz lean ground chicken
- ¼ tbsp tahini
- ½ tsp za'atar
- cup no salt added chickpeas drained and rinsed
- ¼ tbsp Tbsp parsley, chopped

Instructions

1. Set up all of the ingredients on the table.
2. 2 tbsp water in a pan over medium-high heat. Cook the chicken for 5-7 minutes, breaking it up as you stir until it is cooked through. Add the chicken back in. To prevent the pan from drying out, add 1 Tbsp water at a time.
3. Whisk together 3 tbsps of water, tahini, and za'atar in a small bowl.
4. The chicken should be topped with the sauce at this point.
5. At the same time that the sauce and chickpeas are being added to the chicken,
6. Remove from heat and whisk in parsley.
7. Remove from the heat after processing the contents in a food processor until smooth.
8. To enjoy, take one serving and place it in the middle of your plate.

Nutrition Facts

- Calories 89
- Total Fat 4.6g 8%
- Sodium 127.6mg 6%
- Total Carbohydrate 2g 1%
- Sugars 0.1g
- Protein 9g 18%

49. PUREED CHICKEN SALAD

Ingredients

- 1 chicken breast cooked
- 2 Tbsps plain Greek-style yogurt
- 2 Tbsps Light Mayonnaise
- 1/8 tsp celery salt
- 1/8 tsp onion powder
- pinch of black pepper

Instructions

Put the chicken breast in the food processor and pulse until smooth.

Grind the chicken in a food processor until it is a fine powder.

Be sure to incorporate all of the ingredients before serving.

Nutrition

- 84 calories
- 9 grams of carbohydrate,
- 10 grams of protein.
- 4 grams of fat,

50. CHICKEN AND SWEET POTATO PUREE

- prep:10 mins
- cook:20 mins
- total:30 mins
- Servings:28
- Yield:1-3/4 cups of

Ingredients

- 1 chicken breast half, skinless and boneless, 6 ounces
- One large sweet potato, peeled and diced (about 12 ounces)

Instructions

1. Cook chicken breast half for 15 minutes or until no longer pink on the inside (internal temperature should be 170°F) in a small pot with enough boiling water to cover. Cool after removing from heat source. Remove from heat source.
2. Cook the sweet potato for 20-25 minutes, covered, in a small amount of boiling water in a medium saucepan. Cook sweet potatoes according to package directions, then drain and save the cooking liquid. To fully mash potatoes, use a fork or a potato masher.
3. Food processor or mini-food mill to grind chicken. Sweet potatoes and chicken mashed up together. Depending on how thick your child prefers their pudding, you may need to add up to 1 cup of the remaining cooking liquid. Use right away or place in the freezer for up to three months.

To Freeze:

Fill ice cube trays halfway with completed food and freeze. Place waxed paper over top and place in the freezer to set. When ice cubes are frozen, remove them from the tray and place them in a freezer bag or a resealable container with plastic wrap. Indicate the contents and date of the package on the label. Use within a month after purchasing the item. Thaw overnight in the refrigerator before serving.

To Serve:

In a small dish set over boiling water, reheat the thawed mixture until it is lukewarm. Serve with a little more sauce, which you may stir in. To ensure that the food is not very hot, always take a little bite.

Nutrition Facts

- 20 calories,
- 3 mg of cholesterol,
- 3 grams of carbs,
- one gram of sugar,
- 1 gram of protein.

51.   BANANA, TOFU + PEAR BABY FOOD PUREE

- Yield: 10 ounces
- Prep: 5 minutes

Ingredients

- 1 banana
- 1/2 cup tofu
- 1 pear, peeled, cored, and roughly chopped

Instructions

1. I am placing the tofu on a board and dabbing with a paper towel or burp cloth to remove excess water. After roughly cubing, add to a blender or food processor.
2. Blend or process the pears and bananas together in a large food processor or blender. Puree for 1-2 minutes, adding 1/4 cup water at a time, until perfectly smooth.

Notes

Age: 6+ months

Yield: 10 ounces

Note on Tofu: For these dishes, I recommend using organic, sprouted firm tofu. Soybeans can be ultra-processed, yet spouted soybeans are gentler on a baby's tummy.

Storage: For 3-4 days in the fridge, place an airtight jar with the salsa. Freezer – up to four months of storage (this and this are my favorite freezer storage containers).

52.   CHEESY CAULIFLOWER PUREE

- Under 30 minutes
- for 4 servings

Ingredients

- 1 head cauliflower
- salt, as need
- 2 tbsps butter
- ¼ cup whole milk (60 mL)
- pepper, as need

- 1 cup white cheddar cheese (100 g), + more for garnish
- fresh chive, chopped

Preparation

1. Prepare the cauliflower by chopping it into florets.
2. Medium-high heat a medium-sized pot of water until it's boiling. Boil the cauliflower for 15 minutes or until it is soft and tender when pierced with a fork.
3. Return the cauliflower to the pot when it has been drained.
4. To the cauliflower, add salt, butter, and milk.
5. In a large bowl, mash all ingredients until smooth and creamy.
6. Stir in the pepper and the cheddar cheese until everything is well-mixed together.
7. Mix in the chives after you've added everything else.
8. Add chives and extra cheddar cheese before serving.
9. Enjoy!

53. BASIC OATMEAL

- Prep Time: 10 mins
- Cook Time: 5 mins
- Total Time: 15 minutes
- Yield: 2 bowls

Ingredients

- 1 cup (90g) old-fashioned oats
- 1 cup (240 ml) milk or vegetable milk
- 1 cup (240 ml) water
- A pinch of salt
- ¼ tsp cinnamon
- Maple syrup (optional)

Instructions

1. In a small bowl, bring to a boil with milk and water.
2. Once simmering, add oats, salt, and cinnamon as needed.
3. Cook uncovered for 3–5 minutes until thickened.
4. Turn off the heat. Remove from heat and cool before using.
5. Serve with chosen toppings and maple syrup*, and divide evenly between two bowls.

54. PEPPERMINT MILKSHAKE

- Prep Time 5 minutes
- Total Time 5 minutes
- Servings 2

Ingredients

- 2 cups of vanilla ice cream
- 1/2 cup milk
- 1/4 cup candy cane crushed
- 1 tsp peppermint extract
- whipped cream

Instructions

1. Blend all ingredients, including ice cream and milk, until smooth.
2. Add all ingredients to a large mixing bowl and stir until well-mixed
3. Then, add whipped cream and crushed candy canes to a glass and serve.

Nutrition Facts

- Calories from Fat: 425 Calories
- Cholesterol (64 mg):
- 21% Sodium (132 mg/dl)
- 6% 343 mg potassium 10% of the total
- Carbohydrates (61g/20%)
- Sugar (52g)

55. LEMON CRYSTL SHAKE

- Serves 2

Ingredients

- 1/4 cup fresh lemon juice
- 4 tsps sugar
- 1/4 tsp freshly grated lemon rind
- 2 jiggers (3 ounces) Cuarenta Y Tres (Spanish herbal liqueur)
- 1 jigger (1 1/2 ounces) vodka

Instructions

1. Lemon juice, sugar, rind, and 1 1/4 cups of water should be mixed in a bowl and whisked until the sugar is dissolved. Fill an ice tray halfway with the mixture and freeze until solid. The lemon combination can be made up to this point, and stored in the refrigerator, for up to 1 day.
2. Blend Cuarenta Y Tres, vodka, and the frozen lemon mixture in a blender until smooth, but the combination is still frozen. Fill two stemmed glasses half-full with the mixture and serve.

56. ORANGE TEA

- Prep/Total Time: 25 min.
- Makes 8 servings (2 quarts)

Ingredients

- 7 cup water
- one can (12 ounces) frozen orange juice concentrate
- 1/2 cup sugar
- 2 tbsps lemon juice
- 5 tsps instant tea
- 1 tsp whole cloves

Directions

Mix the water, orange juice concentrate, sugar, lemon juice, and tea in a big pot and bring to a boil. Make a tiny cheesecloth bag out of the cloves and place it in the saucepan. Cook for 15 - 20 mins with the lid off. Take out the spice bag and set it aside. Serve immediately. Refrigerate any leftovers in a glass jar.

Nutrition Facts

2mg *sodium,* 29g *carbohydrates* (0 *fiber,* 28g *sugars*), 1 gram *protein* in 1 cup: 118 *calories.* 1 cup: 0 *saturated fat,* 0 *cholesterol,* 2mg *sodium* in 1 cup.

57. PUREED VEGETABLE

- prep:15 mins
- total:45 mins
- Servings:6

Ingredients

- Ingredient Checklist
- 2 tbsps olive oil
- 1 onion, coarsely chopped
- Coarse salt and ground pepper
- Vegetable of choice, such as butternut squash (see below for quantities and other options)
- 1 can (14.5 ounces) reduced-sodium chicken broth
- 1 to 3 tsps fresh lemon juice

Instructions

1. Heat the oil in a large Dutch stove or saucepan on medium heat. Add the onion at this point. Add salt and simmer for 5 - 7 minutes, stirring regularly, until softened.
2. Fill the pot with enough water to cover vegetables, broth, and liquid (about 4 to 5 cups of). Cook for 20 mins at a simmer or until the vegetables are tender.
3. Transfer the pureed broth and vegetables to a clean pot once every batch is completed. Fill blender only halfway to prevent spattering and let heat escape: Dishtowel over lid after removing the cap from lid hole. If the soup is excessively thick, thin it with a bit of water. Add a squeeze of lemon juice and salt & pepper to your liking before serving.

Cook's Notes
What Vegetable Should You Eat?

2 1/2 pounds of a parsnip, peeled and sliced into 1-inch pieces.

1 large carrot, peeled and sliced into 1-inch pieces: 2 1/2 pounds

There should be 2 pounds of broccoli (florets alone) and 1 baked potato (peeled and cut into 1-inch slices), both of which should be sliced into bite-sized pieces.

Prepare 2 pounds of celery root, peeled and sliced into 1-inch-thick pieces.

Peeled and sliced into 1-inch pieces, 2 pounds of beets.20 ounces trimmed and quartered button mushrooms + 1 peeled and 1-inch chunked baked potato3 pounds of peeled, seeded, and 1-inch-thick slices of butternut squash.

2 1/2 pounds of cored and floreted cauliflower.

Chopped celery into 1-inch slices and add 1 baked potato, which should be peeled and cut into 1-inch sections.

STAGE 3: SEMI-SOLID/SOFT FOODS

1. HIGH PROTEIN DEVILED EGG AND BACON

- Yields8 Servings
- Prep Time8 mins
- Total Time8 mins

Ingredients

- 8 eggs, hard-boiled and peeled
- three tbsp No salt added chickpeas, rinsed and drained
- ½ cup Low-fat plain Greek yogurt
- 1 tbsp Dijon mustard
- ¼ tsp Paprika
- 2 slices bacon, cooked and crumbled
- 2 tbsp Dill, chopped

Instructions

1. Every egg should be halved lengthwise before assembling. Remove the yolks with care. Make a food processor out of the remaining yolks after discarding half of them. Mix together chickpeas, Greek yogurt, dijon mustard and half of the dill in 1 tbsp of water. Process in a food processor on and off until completely smooth.
2. Trim the bottom of every white so it rests flat before slicing a sliver off the bottom. Place the ingredients in a bowl and stir until well mixed.
3. Fill every egg white with the yolk mixture by spooning or piping it in. Add paprika, bacon crumbles, and the last of the dill as needed.

Nutrition Facts

- Calories 77.3
- Total Fat 1.2g6 percent Saturated Fat
- 33 percent of the population
- 182.5 milligrams of Sodium
- 2.5 grams (1 percent) of total carbohydrates
- Sugars 1.1 grams

2. BAKED RICOTTA FLORENTINE

- Prep Time 10 mins
- Cook Time 15 mins
- Servings: 4

Equipment

- Food chopper
- Saute Pan
- Ramekins

Ingredients

- olive oil spray extra virgin
- 1/4 cup fresh spinach, chopped fine
- 2 tbsp minced sun-dried tomatoes
- 8 oz. ricotta cheese total fat or part-skim
- 1/2 cup shredded mozzarella cheese
- 2 tbsp grated Parmesan cheese

Instructions

1. Set the Stove to 350°F and prepare the food.
2. Cover the insides of your ramekins with olive oil.
3. Heat a medium-sized saute pan with a spray of olive oil.
4. Sauté the chopped spinach until it has wilted in a skillet over medium heat.
5. Mix the ricotta, mozzarella, parmesan, spinach, and sun-dried toadstools in a medium bowl.
6. Grease ramekins and divide the mixture evenly among them.
7. Add more shredded mozzarella to every ramekin before serving.
8. 15 to 20 minutes in the Stove, or until the cheese has melted and started to color somewhat.

Notes

- Utilize ramekins with a capacity of 4-8 ounces—ramekins with measuring lines to assist you in portion control.
- Ricotta cheese can be total fat or part-skim, depending on personal preference. I use part-skim milk to help with calorie reduction.
- Ensure that the ramekins are greased with oil. I use olive oil spray or olive oil infused with garlic or other herbs to improve the flavor.
- A food processor will assist you in finely chopping the sundried tomatoes.

- You can prepare baked ricotta ahead of time and then bake or reheat in the microwave or oven when ready to serve.

Nutrition

- 158 kcal
- 11g protein,
- 7g fat,
- 42mg cholesterol,
- 180 mg sodium,
- 1g sugar

3. SPINACH SOUP WITH LEMON

- Serves: 4
- The time needed: 40 mins

Ingredients

- For the soup:
- 2 tbsp olive oil
- 1 small onion, diced
- 1 garlic clove, minced
- 450 g | 4 cups of frozen spinach, thawed and chopped
- 600 ml vegetable stock
- 3 tbsp butter
- 2 tbsp plain flour
- 400 ml whole milk
- 200 ml double cream
- 1 lemon, juiced
- Salt
- Freshly ground black pepper
- To serve:
- 1 baguette, cut into slices
- Extra-virgin olive oil for brushing
- Crushed red peppercorns
- 2 lemons, cut into wedges

Method:

1. You'll receive your daily dose of greens with this healthy spinach and lemon soup, which is best eaten with crispy, crunchy bread. Add a few red peppers and a wedge of lemon for some extra pizazz and zing.
2. In a big, medium-sized saucepan, heat the olive oil until it shimmers.
3. Simmer for 5 minutes with the onion, garlic, and a pinch of salt. Add the spinach and stock and bring to a gentle simmer while you make the roux—Cook for a few minutes.
4. Butter should be melted in a medium pot over low heat. Cook the roux until it turns a light beige color, about 2 minutes after adding the flour.
5. Whisk in the milk and cream one at a time until well mixed. Simmer for a few minutes before adding to the spinach combination.
6. Reheat the soup and serve. To break up the texture, lightly purée it in a blender or food processor. Add lemon juice, salt, and pepper as needed.
7. Prepare the grill by turning it too high. Sprinkle with sea salt and cook until golden brown.
8. Grill for 2-3 minutes, rotating once, until brown and crisp on the edges. After you've finished grilling, remove the meat and set it aside to cool.
9. Warm the bowls of soup in the microwave for 30 seconds, then spoon them in. Crush some red peppercorns on top, then serve with lemon wedges on the side for squeezing over the top of the baguette slices.

4. PULLED PORK TACO SOUP

- Yield: 6 people
- Prep Time 5 mins
- Cook Time 25 mins
- Total Time 30 mins

Ingredients:

- 1 pound cooked pulled pork
- 1 (15-oz) can wash and drained pinto beans
- 1 (15-oz) can wash and drained black beans
- 1 (10-oz) can Rotel tomatoes, undrained
- 1 (1-oz) packet Ranch dressing mix
- 1 (1-oz) packet taco seasoning
- 1 cup frozen corn
- 5 cups of chicken broth

Instructions:

1. Then add the other ingredients to the Dutch oven and bake for an additional 15 minutes.
2. Set a high heat and bring the mixture to a rapid boil. For 20-30 minutes, reduce heat to a simmering temperature.
3. Make sure to serve with a side of Fritos, cheese, and sour cream if desired.

5. GREEK YOGURT PARFAIT

- prep:10 mins
- total:10 mins
- Yield:8 servings

Ingredients

- 4 cups of nonfat plain Greek yogurt
- 1 cup sucralose granules
- 1?½ tsp vanilla extract
- 2 cups of granola cereal
- 8 cups of frozen mixed fruit, no sugar added

Directions

Pour the yogurt, sweetener, and vanilla extract into a large mixing basin and stir until well blended. Make a thorough stir.

Fill each of the eight plastic glasses with one cup of frozen fruit. Give the yogurt mixture a final topping of half a cup to every one of the cups. Refrigerate until ready to use.

Before eating, sprinkle 1/4 cup granola over the top of every cup of fruit and yogurt.

6. BANANA SPINACH PROTEIN SMOOTHIE

- Prep Time 5 mins
- Total Time 5 mins
- Servings 1 smoothie

Ingredients

- 1 tbsp almond butter
- cup Greek yogurt
- ½ banana
- ¾ cup water
- 1 scoop vanilla protein powder
- 1 huge handful of spinach

Instructions

Blend all ingredients until desired consistency is revered in a blender.

Notes

Want to make a batch of smoothies? Freeze individual portions in jars or freeze ice cube trays with particular ingredients and pop in the blender when the smoothie craving hits.

Nutrition

- 365 calories are in one serving.
- 26 grams of carbohydrates
- 46 grams of protein
- 10 grams of fat
- 13 grams of sugar

7. MOCHA JAVA

- 10 min Prep Time
- 10 min Total Time
- 2 servings

Ingredients

- 2 cups of strong hot coffee
- 1/3 cup instant hot cocoa mix
- 2 tbsp sugar
- 1/4 tsp ground cinnamon, if desired

- 3/4 cup Land

How to make

1. Prepare 2 quarts of coffee in a saucepan. Stir in the cocoa mix, sugar, and optional 1/4 tsp. Cinnamon until dissolved. Add the half-and-half last. Cook for 2-3 minutes until heated through on medium heat, stirring periodically.
2. Add whipped cream to every serving and, if preferred, chocolate shavings and ground cinnamon.

Nutrition (1 serving)

- There are 400 calories in one serving.
- 230 milligrams of Sodium (mg)
- 86 grams of carbs (g)
- 4 Fibre in the Diet 6 Lean Protein (g)

8. BERRY AVOCADO SMOOTHIE

- Yield: 1 serving
- Prep Time: 5 minutes
- Total Time: 5 minutes

Ingredients

- 2 1/2 avocados (2 1/2 oz.)
- 1 1/4 cup (1 1/4 oz) blueberries
- 1 pound of strawberries (5 oz)
- 1/2 cup Greek yogurt (2% fat) (4 oz)
- 1/2 cup low-fat milk (4 oz)
- 1 tsp raw honey, optional

Instructions

1. Then blend in the fruits and yogurt with the milk until smooth.
2. Blend the ingredient in a blender until they are entirely smooth.
3. If using honey, taste before adding more.
4. Serve immediately or store cold for up to two days in the refrigerator.

Nutrition Information:

Servings Per Container:

- 1 There are 352 calories
- in a serving.
- 16 grams of fat
- 154 milligrams of Sodium
- 39 grams of carbs
- Total Carbohydrates:
- 9 grams 35 grams of sugar
- 22g of protein

9. TUSCAN WHITE BEAN SOUP

- Prep Time: 10 minutes
- Cook Time: 20 minutes
- Total Time: 30 minutes
- Yield: 4 servings

Ingredients

- 2 tbsp olive oil
- 3 shallots, finely chopped
- 2 garlic cloves, chopped
- 1 large carrot, chopped x
- 1 large celery stalk, chopped
- 1 19oz can cannellini beans
- 1 sprig rosemary
- 1 tsp Provence herbs (can sub some dried thyme or oregano)
- a half teaspoon of red chili flakes (optional for spice)
- 1 litre low-sodium vegetable broth
- salt & pepper as need
- 1 cup kale, stems removed and chopped.

Instructions

1. Add the shallots to the hot olive oil and season with salt and pepper. On medium heat, sauté for 1-2 minutes, then add the garlic and cook for another minute.
2. Cook the carrots and celery for 5 minutes over medium-high heat or until they are soft. Add salt and pepper as needed.
3. Incorporate the cannellini bean and rosemary, herbs de Provence, and chili flakes into the stock, bringing to a boil, then decreasing heat to a gentle simmer and covering for 15 minutes, until the beans are tender.
4. The rosemary sprig can be removed, and the soup is transferred to a blender (or hand blender) and blended until smooth. Re-incorporate into the soup and thoroughly mix.
5. Stir in the greens until it's wilted before serving.
6. If you'd like, garnish the soup with fresh herbs and chile flakes.

Notes

- Preheat the saucepan before adding the oil. This will assist in preventing stickiness.
- In this dish, shallots replace onions. Shallots have a more prosperous, butterier flavor, making for a more delightful soup!
- Don't skip browning the vegetables. This adds flavor to the soup.
- No need to blend any of it. However, mixing 1/3 of it makes it creamier. This soup is deliciously blended or not!
- Cannellini beans are used in this dish, but any white bean can be used.

Nutrition

- 160 calories
- 290 milligrams of Sodium 7g fat,
- 18g carbohydrates
- 5.4g of fiber
- 8g of protein

10. CHOCOLATE CHERRY SMOOTHIE

- Prep Time: 5 min
- Total Time: 5 min
- Yield: Serves 2

Ingredients

- 2 cups of frozen cherries
- one cup unsweetened almond milk (plain or vanilla)
- 2 tbsp raw cacao powder (cocoa powder is ok too)
- 1 small Medjool date (pitted and chopped) or 1 tsp pure maple syrup, optional
- 1 scoop protein powder (plain or vanilla) or 2 tbsps almond butter, optional

optional toppings

- granola
- cacao nibs
- hemp hearts

Instructions

1. Add full ingredients to a blender and blend until smooth, adding more milk if necessary.
2. Eat or drink with a spoon and an optional topping. Could you take pleasure in it frequently?
3. This recipe serves one hearty serving or two smaller ones.

Notes

- Substitute 1 frozen banana or 12 cups of fresh cherries for the frozen ones. Begin with 12 cups milk and add extra as needed. To make it more decadent, use light coconut milk from a can! Make it raw with water or almond milk.

11. TURKEY KALE MEATBALLS

- Prep Time 5 minutes
- Cook Time 20 minutes
- Total Time 25 minutes
- Servings 20 meatballs

Ingredients

- 1 pound lean ground turkey
- 2 cups of packed chopped kale (50 grams)
- 2 oz. Pecorino Romano cheese, freshly grated (56 grams)
- 1/8 cup chopped fresh parsley
- 1 large egg
- 2 tsp garlic powder
- salt and pepper, as need

Instructions

1. Warm a significant cast-iron skillet medium heat, adding a little oil if needed.
2. In a pot, mix the ground turkey with the greens and season with salt and pepper (using your hands works best).
3. Mix in the egg until everything is well-integrated.
4. Make a last addition of cheese and blend well.
5. Salt and pepper as needed. Mix all ingredients well. Add parsley and garlic powder as needed.
6. Form tbsp full of the turkey mixture into balls and fry in a skillet over medium heat until golden brown.
7. Cook for 20-25 minutes, tossing regularly until browned on both sides and no pink remains in a cast-iron skillet.
8. Serve and take pleasure in!

Notes

- These can also be baked - preheat oven to 350 degrees F, prepare a baking sheet with parchment paper, and bake for approximately 20-25 minutes, or until firm and without a pick.

Nutrition Facts

- Meatballs with Kale and Turkey Calories Per Serving (5 meatballs)
- 202 calories are the number of calories in one serving. calories from fat (55%) fat (6.1g) (9% of daily value)
- 400 milligrams of Sodium, or 18 percent

- Carbohydrates 24.41 grams to one percent
- Fiber 0.2g of the total
- 34.2g68 percent of your diet should be protein.

12. BUFFALO CHICKEN MEATBALLS

- Prep: 15 min.
- Bake: 20 min.
- Makes 2 dozen

Ingredients

- 3/4 cup bread crumbs (panko)
- 1/3 cup + 1/2 cup hot sauce from Louisiana, divided
- 1/4 cup celery, chopped
- 1 large egg white
- 1 pound lean ground chicken
- Optional: Reduced-fat ranch salad dressing or reduced-fat blue cheese salad dressing and chopped celery leaves

Directions

1. Turn the Stove on to 400 degrees Fahrenheit and prepare the oven. Mix bread crumbs, celery, and 1/3 cup hot sauce in a large basin. Add the chicken and toss to mix, being careful not to overmix.
2. Make 24 1-inch balls out of the dough. Put in a shallow baking pan on a greased rack. Bake for 20 minutes. Put the pan in the oven and bake for 20-25 minutes, or until the chicken is done.
3. Toss remaining hot sauce with meatballs before serving. Sprinkle with celery leaves and serve with salad dressing, if preferred.

Nutrition Facts

- 35 calories,
- 1g fat (0 saturated fat),
- 14 mg cholesterol,
- 24mg sodium (including the salt),
- and 2g carbohydrate

13. RICOTTA SCRAMBLED EGGS

- Prep Time: 5 minutes
- Cook Time: 5 minutes
- Total Time: 10 minutes
- Yield: 1

Ingredients:

- 2 eggs
- 1/2 cup milk
- 1/2 cup ricotta at room temperature
- 1 tbsp chopped fresh chives
- Sea salt and pepper

Instruction :

1. Mix the eggs and milk in a big bowl and whisk until well mixed (I also like to scramble eggs by shaking the eggs and the milk vigorously in a mason jar).
2. Eggs should be scrambled in a medium nonstick skillet over medium heat. Cook, gently stirring. Sometimes, until the eggs are just starting to set.
3. Just before the eggs are done, add the ricotta and fresh herbs and gently fold them in. Try a bite and season with salt and pepper if desired.
4. Serve immediately after being transferred to a bowl!

Nutrition Facts

Serves Serving Size:

1 Calorie; 36 Percent 148 percent of total fat: 28.1 grams of saturates, 15 grams of trans fat. 445.11 milligrams of cholesterol 314 milligrams of Sodium (13 percent)4% of Total Carbohydrates are from Fiber Fibre in the diet: 0.1 grams Sugars: 7 grams 61 percent of the population 30.7 grams of protein

14. ZUCCHINI SOUP

- Prep Time: 15 minutes
- Cook Time: 35 minutes
- Total Time: 50 minutes
- Servings: 6

Ingredients

- 2 Tbsps butter
- 1 small yellow onion, diced
- 2 cloves garlic, minced
- ¼ tsp dried rosemary
- ¼ tsp dried thyme
- ¼ tsp celery salt
- ¼ tsp black pepper
- ¼ tsp kosher salt
- 1 pinch cayenne, optional
- 5 cups of zucchini, cut into chunks
- 3 cups of chicken broth
- 1 Tbsp soy sauce (or Worcestershire sauce)
- 2 Russet potatoes (equivalent to 1 pound)
- 1/2 cup heavy cream or half-and-half
- 1 cup Cheddar Cheese

Instructions

1. If your zucchini gets huge, you may want to peel it before using it in this soup because the skins may be rough and bitter.
2. For optimum results, use a block of cheese and shred it. Set aside for a few minutes so it can cool to room temperature before using. When it's melted, it'll go gently into the soup.
3. In a medium-sized soup pot, melt butter until smooth. Continue cooking for another five minutes, stirring occasionally. Add onions, garlic and continue cooking until softened, another five minutes. Cook for a further 30 seconds after adding the garlic.
4. Dissolve 1/8 tsp of cayenne pepper in water, then add to the zucchini along with the rest of the ingredients. 5 minutes of sautéing is sufficient.
5. The potatoes should be peeled and rinsed. So they cook evenly and quickly, cut them up into small, equal-sized chunks.

6. Chicken broth and soy sauce can be added, along with diced potatoes. Place on high warm and bring to a boil, then lower to a medium-low setting. If necessary, wipe any dark foam at the top of the container using a spatula.
7. Cook covered for twenty mins or until vegetables are very soft. Approximately a quarter-hour
8. Take it off the heat. Blend until sleek with an immersion blender or in batches in a blender.

Optional:

- Return to low heat. Add the half-and-half.
- Stir in the cheese slowly. Serve hot or cold!

Nutrition

- 226kcal of energy in it.
- 20 grams of carbohydrate
- 9 grams of protein
- 13 grams of fat

15. SLOW COOKER CHICKEN CURRY

- Prep: 15 mins
- Cook: 5 hrs
- Total: 5 hrs 15 mins
- Servings: 4 servings

Ingredients

- 1 large sweet potato scrubbed and diced into 1/2-inch pieces
- 2 red bell peppers cored and thinly sliced
- 1/4 cup water
- 2 limes, freshly squeezed
- 2 tbsp curry powder
- 2 tsps smoked paprika
- 1 tsp ground cumin
- 1 tsp ground chili powder
- 1 tsp kosher salt
- one 1/2 pounds boneless, skinless chicken thighs
- 1 tbsp extra virgin olive oil
- 1 can light coconut milk 14 ounces; (for a thicker, creamier sauce, use regular coconut milk)

- two tbsp cornstarch mixed with 3 tbsp water to create a slurry
- For serving: prepared brown rice or quinoa; chopped fresh cilantro

Instructions

1. Fill the bottom of a 5-quart or larger slow cooker with sweet potatoes and bell peppers. Douse with water and squeeze in lime juice after you've done this.
2. Mix the curry powder, smoked paprika, cumin, and chili powder with the salt in a small bowl. Spread the chicken thighs out on a big platter or cutting board and coat both sides with roughly two-thirds of the spice mixture. Set aside the remaining spice mixture once you've rubbed the chicken with it to cover it.
3. Melt the coriander leaves in a large pan over medium heat. Add the olive oil and heat through. Pan-sear the chicken thighs for about 2 minutes on every side once the oil is hot and glistening. Do the same for the other side. In the slow cooker, place the seared chicken on top of the vegetables. Add the rest of the spice mixture on top. Cook the chicken covered for 4 to 5 hours on low (or 2 to 3 hours on high) or until it is thoroughly done. An instant-read thermometer should read 165°F if you're successful.
4. Cut the chicken thighs in half lengthwise and remove them from the slow cooker. Cut the chicken into bite-sized pieces or shred it with two forks when it's cold enough to handle. Separate yourself from the situation.
5. Stir in the coconut milk and cornstarch slurry with the veggies and boiling liquid in the slow cooker. The sauce should be slightly thickened by the time you every the end of the 15-minute cooking time. Stir the sauce and chicken together in the slow cooker, then return the chicken to it. Cook the veggies and chicken for another 15 minutes, covered, on the stovetop, until hot and tender. Serve warm over rice, quinoa, or naan, garnished with fresh cilantro.

Nutrition

- 22 grams of carbs
- 35g of protein
- 18 grams of fat
- 4 grams of dietary fiber
- 4 grams of sugar

16. BAKED FISH WITH ALMOND CHUTNEY

- Yields 8 Servings
- Prep Time 5 mins
- Cook Time 20 mins
- Total Time 25 mins

Ingredients

- one lb Flaky white fish (tilapia, flounder, etc.)
- one tbsp Olive oil
- 2 tsp Lemon juice
- ½ cup Sliced raw almonds
- ½ cup No salt added diced tomatoes
- 1 tsp Coriander

Instructions

1. Preheat the oven to 375 degrees Fahrenheit.
2. Toss the olive oil and lemon juice in a large casserole dish until well mixed and smooth.
3. Dry the fish with a paper towel. Toss the fish in the olive oil mixture before adding it to the casserole. Make a thin coating and then spread it out evenly. Bake for 15 - 20 minutes, or until the fish flakes easily when tested with a fork. The thickness of the meat will affect cooking time.
4. Mix almonds, diced tomatoes, and coriander in a food processor or high-speed blender. Chop and mix ingredients in a food processor or blender. Chunky is best when it comes to the mixture.
5. Remove the fish from the stove and serve it with the chutney that has been spooned on top. Cook for an additional 2-3 mins, or until the sauce is heated through and the fish is flaky.

17. CRANBERRY, SAGE, AND GRUYERE TURKEY MEATBALLS

- Prep Time 5 mins
- Cook Time 20 mins
- Total Time 25 mins
- Servings: 16 meatballs

Ingredients

- 1 pound lean ground turkey
- 1/3 cup breadcrumbs plain
- 1 egg
- 1/3 cup Gruyere shredded
- 1/3 cup dried cranberries no sugar added
- Pinch of salt
- 1/8 tsp black pepper
- 1/4 tsp dried sage
- Prepared turkey gravy

Instructions

1. Set the oven to 350°F.
2. Spray olive oil on a baking sheet to prevent sticking.
3. Turkey should be mixed with the gruyere cheese as well as the cranberries and breadcrumbs.
4. To create 1-1/2 ounce meatballs, scoop out roughly 1 1/2-2 tbsps of the meat mixture and roll into a ball.
5. Place the turkey meatballs on a baking sheet that has been preheated.
6. Put in the oven and bake for 15-20 minutes or until the internal temperature of the meatball reverses 165 degrees Fahrenheit.
7. Serve with gravy, whether it's your own or store-bought.

Notes

For more moisture, bake meatballs for about 10 minutes in the oven, then transfer to a saucepan and cover with gravy. Heat the meatballs in gravy for the remaining 10 minutes or until cooked through.

Nutrition

- 172 calories per serving (3 meatballs),
- 11.7 grams of carbohydrates,
- 21.4 grams of protein,
- 4.6 grams of fat,

18. JUICE JELLY / JELLO POTS

- Serves 8
- Prep 20 mins

Ingredients

- 3 tsp McKenzie's Gelatine Powder
- 1L Orange Juice (Fresh or UHT)

Directions

1. 1/4 of the juice and the gelatine powder should be mixed well in a medium bowl.
2. The remaining juice should be warmed but not boiled in the meantime.
3. Place cold gelatine in a mixing bowl and add hot juice. Stir until gelatine powder is completely dissolved, about 2 minutes. Remove from heat.
4. Place jelly in a container or mold of your choice and refrigerate overnight to set.

Tips

- This procedure also works with other juices like Orange & Mango, Apple Juice, and Berry Juice.

19. SPINACH AND FETA BAKE

- READY IN: 55mins
- SERVES: 4

INGREDIENTS

- one(10 ounces) package frozen spinach (thawed and squeezed dry)
- 1 cup cottage cheese

DIRECTIONS

1. Except for 1 tsp. Parmesan cheese, mix all the ingredients in a large bowl.
2. Then pour into a greased baking dish and top with the remaining Parmesan cheese, if desired.
3. At 350 degrees, bake for 45-50 minutes, stirring every 10 minutes.

NUTRITION INFO

- PER SERVING percent Serving Size: 1 (201) g Servings Per Recipe: 4 TIMELY RETURN
- Total Calories: 225.9 Fat Calories Consumed: 122
- 13.6 g of total fat (20%)
- saturated fat (40%): 8.1 grams
- 40% Cholesterol 144.9 mg
- 31% of sodium, 736.7 milligrams
- carbohydrates (7.6 grams, 2 percent of total calories)
- The fiber in the Diet: 2.6 grams (10 percent)
- grams of sugar, or 11 percent of your total diet.
- grams of protein (or 39 percent)

20. SOFT CARD SALAD

- prep:15 mins
- cook:15 mins
- total:30 mins
- Yield: 8 servings

Ingredients

- ½ cup chopped onion
- ½ cup chopped green bell pepper
- 2 (10 ounce) packages mixed salad greens
- 4 thinly sliced chicken deli meat, chopped
- 1 tomato, chopped
- ¼ tsp onion powder
- 3 dashes of garlic powder
- 1 pinch ground black pepper
- 2 pinches salt
- 3 tbsp balsamic vinaigrette salad dressing

Directions

1. Set aside to cool after microwaving or sautéing onion and bell pepper till tender.
2. Mix the onion, pepper, salad leaves, deli meat, and tomato in a large salad bowl. Add the onion, garlic, black pepper, and salt as needed. Toss everything together and stir well.
3. Toss the salad one last time before serving, and then drizzle on the salad dressing or vinegar as needed.

Nutrition Facts

Per serving, there are 47 calories, 2.7 grams of protein, 5.3 grams of carbs, 2.1 grams of fat, 3.1 milligrams of cholesterol, and 162.7 milligrams of sodium.

21. SPICY VEGETARIAN CHILI

- Prep: 20 minutes
- Cook: 1 hour 20 minutes
- Total: 1 hour 40 minutes
- SERVES 6

Ingredients

- 3 tbsps olive oil
- 1 yellow onion, finely chopped
- 1 red bell pepper, finely chopped
- 2 carrots, peeled and chopped
- 2 celery stalks, finely chopped
- 2 serrano chile, finely chopped
- 2 tsps minced garlic (about 4 cloves)
- 3 tbsp chili powder
- 2 tsp ground cumin
- 1 tsp smoked paprika
- 1 tsp dried oregano
- 1 tsp coarse kosher salt
- 1/4 tsp black pepper
- 3 cups of vegetable broth
- 2 15-ounce cans of fire-roasted diced tomatoes
- 1 15-ounce can rinse and drained red kidney beans
- 1 15-ounce can washed and drained black beans
- 2 tbsps your favorite spicy hot sauce
- 1 tbsp fresh lime juice
- optional toppings
- shredded cheese, sour cream, cilantro, hot sauce

optional toppings

- shredded cheese, sour cream, cilantro, hot sauce

Instructions

1. Large pot or Dutch Stove: Heat oil in a medium-sized saucepan or Dutch oven. Continue to simmer, stirring periodically, for an additional 20 minutes, or until the onions have begun to caramelize.
2. Then add the following: Cook for 10 minutes, stirring regularly, on medium-high heat.
3. Add cumin, paprika, oregano, salt, and black pepper to the chili powder mixture— Cook for one minute after stirring everything together.
4. Chili powder is an excellent addition to this dish because it adds a kick of heat without being overpowering. To boil, mix all ingredients and bring to a boil over high heat. Cook, uncovered, for 45 minutes to an hour on low heat, or until the chili is the right thickness for you. It thickens as it simmers for more extended periods.
5. Remove from the fire, add the lime juice, and season with salt and pepper as needed. If required, add a little more salt to the dish.
6. Scoop into bowls and serve with additional spicy sauce and/or sour cream.

Tips:

To freeze, first, cool the chili down entirely by placing it in the fridge. Once chilled, store in freezer-safe zip-top bags or containers and freeze. When ready to eat, let the frozen container thaw completely in the fridge or defrost in the microwave. Reheat in the stove or in the microwave until completely warm.

Nutrition Information

- 6 Calories in one serving: 266 (13 percent)
- 40 grams of carbohydrates (13 percent)
- 11g of protein (22 percent)
- 8g of fat (12 percent)
- 1445 milligrams of sodium (60 percent)
- 11 grams of sugar (12 percent)

22. AVOCADO CHICKEN POWER SALAD

- PREP TIME 3 mins
- SERVES 1
- TOTAL TIME 3 mins

Ingredients

- 1 cup Minute Ready to Serve Organic White & Red Quinoa
- 1 cup power blend coleslaw mix (Brussels sprouts, Napa cabbage, kohlrabi, broccoli, carrots, and kale)
- 1/2 cup (3 oz) chopped, cooked chicken
- 1/4 avocado, chopped
- 4 cherry tomatoes, halved
- 1 tbsp sliced green onions
- 2 tbsp vinaigrette dressing

Instructions

1. Quinoa, chicken, avocado, and Brussels sprouts in a salad will provide you with the energy you need to go through your day. The salad also contains organic quinoa.
2. A medium bowl holds the unheated quinoa mixture along with the other ingredients.
3. Toss the salad with the vinaigrette to mix the flavors.

23. TACO CASSEROLE

- Prep Time: 10 minutes
- Cook Time: 30 minutes
- Total Time: 40 minutes
- Servings: 6

Ingredients

- 6 tortilla chips or Doritos or other crisp toppings (about 34 cups)
- 1 small yellow onion, diced
- 2 tablespoons taco seasoning, or 1 ounce.
- 16 oz. refried beans
- ¾ cup sour cream, *see notes
- 2 cups of shredded cheddar cheese
- ¼ cup black olives, sliced
- 6 tortilla chips or Doritos or other crisp toppings (about 34 cups)

- To garnish:
- Green onions, (optional)
- 1/3 cup shredded lettuce
- 1/3 cup tomatoes, diced

Instructions

While the beef is cooking, bring the sour cream to room temperature. Because it won't transition from cold to hot as quickly, it won't curdle when baked.

Turn the stove to 350 degrees Fahrenheit.

Stir together the ground beef and diced onions in a large skillet over medium heat, and cook and crumble until the meat is done.

Eliminate any extra grease by rinsing with water.

Taco seasoning and 34 cup of water should be added at this point.

Set a high heat and bring the mixture to a rapid boil.

Stirring occasionally, lower the heat to a simmer and cook for 5 minutes. Take it off the heat.

In a casserole dish, spread the refried beans evenly. In my case, the paper was 9 x 13, but any size will do.)

Then top with sour cream and serve.

Add the cooked ground beef mixture and then the cheese to the top to complete the meal.

Refrigerate it until you're ready to bake it if you're making it ahead of time.

Baking:

If baking right away: Let stand for 15 minutes, then cover with cheese and bake until melted.

If you want to bake the casserole after it's been chilled, follow these instructions:
25 minutes in the oven with the cover on. Bake for a additional 5 minutes after lifting the cover.

Add the toppings:

Black olives and other crunchy garnishes go on top of the casserole. (If desired, top with extra cheese.)

For 8 minutes, bake the dish with the lid off.

Assemble your sandwich and then top with chopped green onions and/or sliced tomatoes before serving!

Notes

Light sour cream might curdle and separate, so stay away from it. When adding it to the casserole, make sure it's at least at room temperature

Nutrition:

- 547 calories
- 24 grams of carbohydrates,
- 28 grams of protein
- 38 grams of fat,
- 1273 milligrams of sodium,
- 5 grams of sugar,

24. SUMMER VEGETABLES WITH SAUSAGE AND POTATOES SKILLET

- Prep Time: 10 mins
- Cook Time: 50 mins
- Total Time: 1 hr
- Yield: 4 servings

Ingredients

- two tsp olive oil
- one lb baby red potatoes, cut in half or quartered
- 1/2 tsp garlic powder
- one tsp kosher salt
- fresh cracked pepper, as need
- 14 oz Italian chicken sausage, sliced 1-inch thick
- one large onion, chopped
- 4 to 5 garlic cloves, crushed with a knife
- 1/2 orange bell pepper, diced 1-inch squares
- 1/2 yellow bell pepper, diced one-inch squares
- one red bell pepper, diced 1-inch squares
- two tbsp fresh rosemary, or another fresh herb such as thyme
- two cups of zucchini, 1/2 inch thick and quartered

Instructions

1. Season potato with garlic powder, salt, and pepper, then fry them covered in oil in a large, deep nonstick skillet over high heat.
2. Reducing heat when the skillet is hot and beginning to crackle is a good time to start shaking the pan to keep the potatoes from burning.
3. Once you've removed them from the heat, let them sit for 5 minutes with the lid on, then transfer them to a serving plate.
4. Cook the sausage for about 10 minutes, stirring periodically, on medium-low heat until it is browned but not fully cooked.
5. Add salt and pepper to the chopped vegetables and toss to mix. In a large skillet, cook the onion until translucent, then add the peppers, garlic, and rosemary.
6. While cooking, make occasional stirs to ensure onions and peppers don't burn.
7. Cook the zucchini for a further 5 minutes, frequently stirring, until it is tender.
8. Put the potatoes back in the skillet and toss thoroughly to mix the flavors. Cover and simmer for an additional five mins after you've made any necessary adjustments with the salt and pepper.

Nutrition

- 307 calories
- 33.5 grams of carbohydrate,
- 21 grams of protein
- 10.5 grams of fat,
- 844 mg of sodium,
- 9.5 grams of sugar.

25.   STRAWBERRY OATMEAL BARS

- Total: 1 hr 20 min
- Prep: 10 min
- Inactive: 30 min
- Cook: 40 min
- Yield: 24 servings

Ingredients

- two sticks (1 cup) salted butter, cut into pieces, + more for greasing pan
- 1 1/2 cups of all-purpose flour
- 1 1/2 cup oats
- 1 cup packed brown sugar
- 1 tsp baking powder
- 1/2 tsp salt
- One 10 to 12-ounce jar of strawberry preserves

Directions

1. Set the stove to 350 degrees Fahrenheit and prepare the casserole. Butter a rectangle baking dish that measures 9 inches by 13 inches.
2. Butter, flour, oats, brown sugar, baking powder, and salt should be mixed together. Half of the oat mixture should be pressed into the pan. Strawberry preserves should be spread on top of the bread. Pat lightly the other half of the oat mixture on top before sprinkling the last half on top. In the stove, bake for 30 to 40 minutes, or until golden brown. Cut into squares once they have cooled fully. Let cool completely before cutting.

26. PINA COLADA PROTEIN SHAKE

- Yield: 1 serving

Ingredients

- 1 cup frozen pineapple chunks
- 1/2 frozen banana (optional)
- 6 ounces unsweetened coconut milk
- 1/2 tsp coconut extract
- 1 scoop vanilla protein powder

Instructions

1. In a large mixing basin, combine all of the ingredients.
2. Cover and blend on high for 10-15 seconds, or until smooth and frosty.
3. Drink up right away from the glass.

Nutrition Information

- 435 37 grams of fat
- 32g 0 milligrams of cholesterol
- 24mg of sodium
- 2 grams of dietary fiber
- 17 grams of sugar
- 4g of protein

27. HIGH PROTEIN CREAMY TACO SOUP

- Yield: 16 servings
- Prep Time: 5 minutes
- Cook Time: 20 minutes
- Total Time: 25 minutes

Ingredients

- 93/7 Ground Turkey, 2 pounds (or your choice of meat)
- 15 oz can Sliced Stewed Tomatoes
- 10 oz can Rotel
- 15 oz. black bean can rinsed and drained
- fifteen oz can Pinto Beans, drained and rinsed
- Corn in a 15-ounce can
- 12 oz bag 3 Pepper & Onion Blend, frozen
- Broccoli and Cauliflower Florets, 12-ounce bag, set (or 1/2 broccoli, 1/2 cauliflower if you can't locate a blend)
- eight oz Fat-Free Cream Cheese, room temp
- Fat-Free Greek Yogurt, 1 C (227g)
- 1 packet Ranch Dip Mix
- 2 packets Taco Seasoning

Instructions

1. Over medium-high heat, brown your choice of ground meat with one package of taco seasoning in a big saucepan or in the Instant Pot. If you're using an Instant Pot, you'll want to use the saute feature instead.)
2. Once the meat has finished cooking, add the rest of the ingredients, including the cauliflower and broccoli, to a big pot. Stirring frequently, bring the mix to a simmer and cook until the frozen vegetables start to soften.

3. Fry the soup for 5-10 minutes, or until all the cream cheese and Greek yogurt are well mixed, and there are no flakes.
4. You can use a food scale to weigh your final combination in a large bowl before portioning it out according to your needs. Portion according to your calorie/macro objectives. You may portion out 16 205-calorie meals, 10 330-calorie meals, 7 470-calorie meals, or whatever works best for your meal frequency and calorie requirements using the total calories (around 3,300). Include any other ingredients you intend to include in the soup, such as cheese, sour cream, or tortilla chips.

Nutrition Information:

- Per 1/16 serving:
- 210 Calories,
- 18g Protein,
- 23g Carbs,
- 5g Fat

28. PUMPKIN SPICE HOT CHOCOLATE

- prep:10 mins
- cook:5 mins
- total:15 mins
- Servings:2

Ingredients

- ½ cup milk
- ? cup heavy whipping cream
- ¼ cup milk chocolate chips
- 1 tsp cocoa powder
- 1?½ tsps pumpkin puree
- ¼ tsp pumpkin pie spice
- ¼ cup whipped cream
- 1 pinch ground cinnamon (optional)
- 1 pinch ground nutmeg (optional)

Directions

1. Over medium heat, mix milk, cream, chocolate chips, and cocoa powder in a saucepan; whisk until smooth, 3 to 5 minutes—mixture in the pumpkin puree and pumpkin pie spice. Add the mashed bananas and mix well.
2. Fill two mugs with hot chocolate and serve immediately. Add whipped cream and cinnamon, and nutmeg to the whipped cream before serving.

Nutrition Facts

- Calories from fat are 64.9mg;
- sodium is 52.6mg;
- protein is 4.2g;
- carbs are 19.5g;
- fat is 24.2g;
- cholesterol is 64.9mg.

29. AFRICAN CHICKEN PEANUT STEW

- Prep Time 20 mins
- Cook Time 115 mins
- Total Time 2 hrs 15 mins
- Servings 6 to 8 servings

Ingredients

- 2 – 3 lb chicken legs, thighs, or
- three tbsps vegetable oil
- 1 large yellow or white onion, sliced
- 3-inch piece of ginger, peeled and minced
- 6-8 garlic cloves, chopped roughly
- 2-3 lb sweet potatoes, peeled and chunked
- 1 15-ounce can of crushed tomatoes
- 1-quart chicken stock
- one cup peanut butter
- 1 cup roasted peanuts
- 1 tbsp ground coriander
- 1 tsp cayenne, or as need
- Salt and black pepper
- 12 cup chopped cilantro

Method

1. To brown the chicken, place a large soup pot over medium-high heat and add the vegetable oil. Pat, the chicken, pieces dry and sear them in oil with salt and pepper. Do this in batches so that you don't overcrowd the pot. As the chicken browns, remove it from the pan and set it aside.
2. Stir-fry the vegetables for 3-4 minutes, scraping up any browned bits from the bottom of the pot as you go. Cook for an additional 1-2 minutes, then add the ginger and garlic and mix well to blend.
3. In a large soup pot, mix all of the ingredients and bring to a boil. Stir in the chicken broth, smashed tomatoes, peanut butter, peanuts, coriander, and cayenne pepper. Put the chicken in the pot and cook it according to the package directions. Bring to a simmer and, if necessary, season with additional salt.
4. Turn off the heat and simmer for 90 minutes, or until the chicken is cooked and the sweet potatoes fall off the bone.
5. Chunk the cooked chicken and remove the bones: Set the chicken pieces aside to chill until they are cool enough to handle. You can either drag and discard the skin or chop it up and re-add it to the stew.
6. Remove the meat from the bones, break it up, and return it to the pan.
7. Salt and cayenne should be adjusted, and then as much black pepper as you can stand should be added—the stew should be spicy. Taste and adjust seasonings. Serve with steamed rice or cilantro as a dipping sauce.

30. SCOTCH EGGS

- Prep:20 mins
- Cook:20 mins
- Makes 4

Ingredients

- 5 large eggs
- 300g good-quality pork sausage, skinned
- 1 tsp black peppercorns, crushed
- 140g cooked ham, shredded
- 25g sage, apple & onion stuffing mix
- 1 tsp chopped sage
- 1 tsp chopped thyme
- 1 tsp chopped parsley
- 100g plain flour, seasoned, + extra for dusting

- 100g dried breadcrumbs
- sunflower oil, for frying
- piccalilli, to serve

Method

1. Once the salted water has come to a boil, add four eggs and cook for 7 minutes and 30 seconds. Using a spoon, remove the avocados and place them in a dish of chilled water (this makes them easier to peel later). Wait until they've cooled before peeling and setting them aside. The water can be heated up to the day ahead of time.
2. Stuffing and herbs can be mixed in a small dish with the sausage and pepper to form four equal balls. Then serve in four equal servings. To make one of the balls as flat as possible, place it between two sheets of cling film and press down firmly. Every fried egg should be lightly floured before the sausagemeat is rolled around it to surround it completely. Do this with all of the eggs at once. To make more sausage balls and fried eggs, simply repeat the previous step.
3. The remaining egg should be beaten and spread out on a platter. Separate the flour from the breadcrumbs and set them aside on two plates. Roll the floured eggs, beaten eggs, and breadcrumbs around the contained eggs. They were prepared up to a day in advance.
4. Heat 5cm of oil in a big pot or wok over medium heat until it reverses 160C on a cooking thermometer, or after 10 seconds in the oil, a few breadcrumbs turn brown. For 8-10 minutes, fry as many eggs as possible in the oil until they're golden brown and crispy. Serve halved with some piccalilli after draining on paper towels.

31. LOW-CARB, HIGH-PROTEIN EGG SALAD

- Prep Time 5 mins
- Cook Time 7 mins
- Total Time 12 mins
- Servings: 2

Ingredients

- 4 hard-boiled egg whites
- 2 hard-boiled whole eggs
- 3 tbsp Greek yogurt
- 1 chopped spring onion

- 1 tsp Dijon mustard
- ½ tsp Rosemary spice
- salt as need
- black pepper as need

Instructions

1. Make a pot of water and put the eggs in it.
2. The 4 egg whites and 2 whole eggs should be peeled and mashed with a fork.
3. Mix the items in a bowl.
4. Mix in the rest of the items in the bowl after you've added them.

Nutrition Information:

- Protein: 30
- Carb: 4
- Fat: 10

32. SMOKED SALMON PATE

- Prep Time 5 mins
- Total Time 5 mins
- Servings: 10

Ingredients

- 2 oz poached salmon 60g
- 2 oz smoked salmon 60g (can use offcuts/pieces)
- 2 tbsp cream cheese (approx 34g)
- 2 tsp lemon juice
- 2 tsp yogurt
- ¼ tsp Dijon mustard
- ⅛ tsp paprika
- 1 pinch salt
- 1 pinch pepper

Instructions

1. Pulse all the ingredients until smooth in a food processor. Make sure everything is well blended by scraping down the edges and pulsing it again if necessary.
2. Serve immediately from the bowl or store in the refrigerator until needed (it will keep a couple of days in the fridge).

Notes

Poaching your own salmon is as simple as adding 1 12in/5cm of water to a small pan, 2 tablespoons of white wine, 1-2 tablespoons of lemon juice, and some salt and pepper to taste—Boil the mixture, covered, over medium-high heat. Add the fish to the sauce and boil for 3–6 minutes, depending on the thickness of the salmon chunks. Remove cooked meat from poaching liquid and cool on a platter.

As long as it hasn't been seasoned with a glaze or anything else, leftover baked or otherwise cooked salmon will work just as well here.

The weight of the salmon, both raw and cooked, is nearly the same.

Nutrition

It has calories, protein and fat, and sodium and potassium, but no sugar or iron. Vitamin A has 51IU of vitamin A, and vitamin C has one milligram of vitamin C. Calcium has five milligrams of vitamin C, and iron has one milligram.

33. CRUSTLESS QUICHE

- Prep: 15 mins
- Cook: 35 mins
- Total: 50 mins
- Servings: 4 servings

Ingredients

FOR THE QUICHE BASE:

- 6 large eggs
- 2/3 cup whole milk
- ¼ cup half-and-half
- ½ tsp kosher salt
- ¼ tsp black pepper
- 1 tsp Dijon mustard optional
- Pinch ground nutmeg optional
- 1 1/2 cups desired mix-ins: Suggestions and ingredient details for a broccoli bacon variant are included below. If you are a little less than or more than 1 1/2 cups, that is acceptable.
- 2/3 cup shredded Gruyère cheese; fontina, sharp cheddar, or smoked mozzarella cheese may be substituted

- 2 tbsps chopped fresh chives

FOR THE MIX-INS*:

- Cooked crumbled bacon
- Chopped and sautéed broccoli
- Caramelized onions
- Cubed leftover ham
- Roasted vegetables

Instructions

1. Preheat the stove to 350 degrees F. Center a rack in the center of the oven. Use nonstick spray to coat a 9-inch pie dish.
2. If applicable, prepare any other ingredients
3. In a big mixing pot, combine the eggs, milk, half-and-half, and seasonings.
4. Distribute the mix-ins evenly over the bottom of the pie plate. Finish with a sprinkling of cheese.
5. Do not rush the pouring of the egg mixture into the baking dish. To collect any drippings, use a rimmed baking sheet. On top, scatter the chives.
6. Bake, the quiche for 35 mins, or until the center is set. The edges should be puffed and golden, and the middle should be cooked through with no visible liquid when a thin, sharp knife is put in the center. Allow for a little cooling period. Make large slices out of the potatoes. Enjoy it while it's still warm.

Notes

- Follow these steps to make the Broccoli Bacon version is shown in this post: 4 thick-cut bacon slices, diced Cook for approximately 8 minutes, or until the pieces are crisp and the fat has rendered, in a pan over medium-low heat. Remove the bacon to a dish lined with paper towels using a slotted spoon. All but 1 tbsp bacon fat should be discarded from the skillet. 2 cups broccoli florets, finely cut, and 1 small red or yellow onion, thinly sliced Sauté for about 10 minutes, or until the onion is soft. Use as indicated in the quiche.
- STORAGE: Keep the quiche refrigerated for up to 3 days in an airtight container.
- REHEATING: Reheat leftovers in the stove at 350 degrees F in a pie dish.
- TO FREEZE: A crustless quiche can be frozen. Wrap the quiche snugly in plastic wrap and freeze for up to 3 months in an airtight freezer-safe storage container. Agree to thaw overnight in the refrigerator before reheating.

Nutrition

Serving size: 1 (out of 4); no additional ingredients needed Calories in one serving: 231 3 grams of carbs 17 grams of protein 17 grams of fat 8g of dietary sat fat 279 milligrams of cholesterol 182 milligrams of potassium 2 grams of sugar Vitamin A (retinol): 750 International Units Take 1 milligram of vitamin C daily. 321 milligrams of calcium are present in one cup of milk. 1 milligram of iron

34. PEANUT BUTTER PROTEIN BARS

- Prep: 15 mins
- Cook: 1 hr
- Total: 1 hr 15 mins
- Servings: 12 bars

Ingredients

- 3/4 cup creamy peanut butter*
- 1/3 cup honey
- 2 tbsps coconut oil
- 2 cups of Bob's Red Mill Gluten-Free Rolled Oats
- 1/2 cup vanilla protein powder about 2 scoops, depending upon your brand
- 3 tbsp flaxseed meal
- 1/4 tsp ground cinnamon
- 1/4 tsp kosher salt
- 1/3 cup mini chocolate chips

Instructions

1. Leave an overhang on two sides of an 8- or 9-inch baking pan to use as handles.
2. Melt the coconut oil in the small saucepan set on low heat. Add the honey and peanut butter and stir until smooth. Heat the water in the bowl over a pot of simmering water until it just begins to bubble. (Don't allow the water to come to a boil, and don't let it go too low in the mixing bowl.) Heat and Shake the mixture until it is completely smooth. Turn off the heat under the pot and remove the bowl from it.
3. The same bowl as the peanut butter combination, combine the oats, protein powder, flaxseed, cinnamon, and salt. To blend, give everything a good stir. At first, the mixture will appear quite dry, but it will come together as you continue to stir. It won't be sticky, but pressing on it should keep it together. While the mixture is

still heated, stir in the chocolate chunks. If necessary, chill the bowl in the refrigerator for a few minutes before continuing. (The chocolate will not melt if the mixture is cooled.) Even if the chocolate chips do melt a little, the bars will still taste great.) Refrigerate for 1 hr or until solid before pressing evenly onto the prepared pan.
4. Transfer the bars to a chopping board by lifting them out of the pan with the parchment handles. Cut into desired size bars and savor.

Notes

- The consistency of the bars will vary depending on the brand of peanut butter you choose. If they're too loose, add a tablespoon or two more oats. If the bars are too dry, add a tablespoon of peanut butter, honey, or even water at a time until they hold together when pressed into the pan.
- Depending on the brand of protein powder you use, the nutritional information will differ. If you want to calculate them with a specific brand, go to myfitnesspal.com and do so for free
- The bars can be stored in the freezer for up to three months or at room temperature for up to a week. I prefer
- to wrap mine separately and then take them out of the freezer as needed. They can be chilled, but I like them at room temperature.

Nutrition

There will be one serving (of 12) calories: 244 26 grams of carbohydrates are found in this serving. 9 grams of protein 14 grams of fat 5 grams of saturated fat 3 grams of dietary fiber 13 grams of sugar

---

35. SWEDE SOUP

- Servings: 6 people
- Prep Time15 mins
- Cook Time45 mins

Ingredients

- ½ swede (rutabaga) (500g)
- 2 parsnips (200g)
- 2 carrots (170g)
- 1 onion (150g)
- 2 tbsp olive oil
- 2 tsp ras el hanout

- 1 tsp oregano (dried)
- 600 ml stock (vegetable or chicken)
- salt & pepper

To serve

- Fresh herbs (chopped)
- drizzle cream, or hemp or flax oil (or a knob of butter)

Instructions

1. To 200°C/400°F/Gas Mark 6, preheat the oven. Vegetables should be peeled and cut into 12-inch cubes.
2. Serve in a roasting dish with a generous sprinkle of salt and oregano, then drizzle with olive oil. Stir to mix the oil and spices and ensure that the veggies are well-coated.
3. 15 minutes of roasting time. After then, take the dish out of the oven and give it a good shake or mix. After 15–25 minutes, the potatoes should be tender and begin to brown around the edges.
4. In a large saucepan, mix the cooked veggies with the remaining ingredients. Save a few pieces for later use as a garnish if desired.
5. To get all the crispy bits from the bottom of the pan, use a spatula or wooden spoon to scrape the stock into the roasting dish.
6. Add the vegetable stock to the pot and heat through.
7. Purée the soup with an immersion blender or a food processor.
8. Adjust the seasoning to your liking by giving the dish a taste and tasting it again.
9. Add a knob of butter to your soup for more richness and creaminess. With just a squeeze of lemon juice, the flavors will be enlivened and made more vibrant.

Notes

- Use whatever root vegetable you can find. Soup with swede and carrots, or swede and parsnips, or whatever you have on hand.
- You may customize the spices. I chose a North African spice blend, but Middle Eastern or Indian blends might also work.
- Refrain from adding stock
- to the pan until it has deglazed. A good cook never wastes flavor!
- So prepare extra soup to freeze. Cool it and pack it into plastic pots. Reheat in the microwave or on the stovetop.
- I prefer topped soup. Yours can be topped with seeds, roasted vegetable cubes, chopped fresh herbs, or plain yogurt.

Nutrition Facts

126 Calories from Fat 45 percent of the Daily Value* for Roasted Swede Soup's Fat 5 grams 8 percent Fat from saturated sources 16% 19% of sodium is found in 437 milligrams. 523mg15 percent of your daily allowance is potassium. 20 grams of carbohydrates 7 % of the population 5 grams or 21% of your diet should consist of fiber. 9 grams of sugar, or 10%, of your diet, 2g4 of total calories, are from protein. Vitamin A: 5796 International Units (IU) = 116% Amount of Vitamin C in 30mg: 36% 79 milligrams of calcium (8 percent) Ferrous 1mg6%

36. CHILI LIME TURKEY BURGERS

- Prep Time: 10 minutes
- Cook Time: 12 minutes
- Total Time: 22 minutes
- Servings: 4 burgers

Ingredients

- One pound Ground Turkey, 93% lean
- Four ounces can Diced Green Chilies -drained very well
- 1 tsp lime zest -about 1 lime
- ½ tsp chili powder -make this a full ½ tsp
- ½ tsp kosher salt
- ¼ tsp onion powder
- ¼ tsp garlic powder
- ¼ tsp black pepper

Instructions

1. Alternatively, preheat your gas grill to medium and add a uniform layer of white-hot charcoal on the grates.
2. All the ingredients should be mixed softly in a mixing basin, with clean hands, until the seasonings and lime zest are uniformly integrated. Overmixing will result in tough burgers.
3. A little-known fact about lime zest: If you use too much, it will stay together in a clump. So that it doesn't all wind up in one burger, equally distribute the lime zest over the turkey.
4. Make 4 identical patties with the ingredients listed above. To make every patty stand out, make a small depression in the center with your thumb. Thus, your burgers will not degenerate into tiny hockey pucks as they cook.

5. Use a bit of olive oil to coat the grill grate and the turkey burgers on both sides. This will prevent the turkey burgers from sticking to the grill while cooking.
6. Grill the turkey burgers for seven minutes on every side, for a total of 14 minutes. The inside temperature should be 165 degrees when they're done. Serve the burgers with the buns on the side once they've rested for 3-5 minutes.

37. CRANBERRY CHICKEN SALAD

- Prep Time: 15 minutes
- Total Time: 45 minutes
- Yield: 6 servings

Ingredients

- 4 cups of diced, cooked chicken breast
- 1 large celery stalk, diced
- 1 – 2 green onions, sliced
- 3/4 cup dried cranberries
- 1/2 cup pine nuts, toasted
- 1/2 cup mayonnaise
- 1/4 – 1/2 tsp dry mustard powder (or 1 – 2 tsp Dijon mustard)
- Salt & pepper, as need

Instructions

1. In a large bowl, combine all ingredients.
2. Use an extra tbsp of mayonnaise if necessary to achieve the desired consistency. If necessary, make adjustments to the seasonings.
3. To get the best flavor, chill for at least 30 minutes before serving.

Nutrition

- Approximately the following is the serving size:
- Calories in 1 serving: 414
- 15 grams of sugar • 194.9 milligrams of sodium
- 23.4 g fat, 3.8 g saturated fat, 19 g carbohydrates, and 2.4 g fiber make up this serving.
- 32.1 grams of protein; 107 milligrams of cholesterol

38. ITALIAN MEATLOAF

- Total: 1 hr 15 min
- Prep: 10 min
- Inactive: 5 min
- Cook: 1 hr
- Yield: 4 servings

Ingredients

- 1/4 cup + 2 tbsps extra-virgin olive oil
- 4 tsps (about 6 cloves) chopped garlic
- 2 medium onions, diced
- 2 red peppers, seeded, small diced
- 1/2 cup chopped basil leaves
- 2 tbsps chopped parsley leaves
- 4 eggs
- 1 tsp salt
- 1/2 tsp black pepper
- 2 cups of grated Parmesan
- 1 1/2 cups of breadcrumbs
- 3 pounds ground beef
- 2 tbsps Worcestershire sauce
- 2 tbsps balsamic vinegar
- 1 cup marinara sauce

Directions

1. Set the oven to 350°F.
2. Garlic should be heated in 1/4 cup of olive oil in a medium saute pan on medium heat. Cook for another 30 seconds with the garlic before adding the peppers and onions. Allow for cooling.
3. Combine the basil, parsley, and eggs in a small bowl; season with salt and pepper. In a separate small bowl, mix the Parmesan and breadcrumbs. Toss the remaining 2 tbsps of olive oil with the remaining ingredients in a large bowl, being careful not to overmix. This includes the meat, herbs, and eggs, as well as the Parmesan and breadcrumbs.
4. If you don't have a loaf pan, form the meat mixture into a loaf on an oiled oven tray or baking dish before putting it in the pan. Spread the marinara evenly on top before serving.

5. Bake for fifty to 60 minutes, or until an instant-read thermometer in the center of the meatloaf registers 160 degrees Fahrenheit. Allow five minutes after removing it from the oven before serving. Slice a pie to serve yourself.

39. CREAMY TUSCAN SHRIMP

- Prep Time 5 mins
- Cook Time 10 mins
- Total Time 15 mins
- Servings 4

Ingredients

- 1 pound shrimp (I used 31-40 count size) thawed & peeled
- 2 tbsps butter
- 1 tsp flour
- 4-5 cloves garlic minced
- 1 cup heavy/whipping cream
- 1/2 tsp lemon juice
- 2 dashes of Italian seasoning
- 1/4 cup sun-dried tomatoes chopped or julienned
- 1 cup (packed) fresh baby spinach
- Handful fresh basil cut into thin strips
- Salt & pepper as needed

Instructions

1. Soften the butter in a large skillet over medium heat. Cook for approximately a minute, constantly stirring until the flour is completely dissolved. Add salt as needed.
2. Cook the garlic for about 30 sec, or until it begins to smell good.
3. Then add the sun-dried tomatoes and the Italian spice and whisk until smooth. 2 minutes of simmering time. If it's bubbling excessively, turn down the heat.
4. Don't overcook the shrimp; instead, cook them for about 5 minutes, or until they're opaque in the middle and the sauce has thickened just a little.
5. Cook for an additional 2 minutes after adding the spinach and basil. If necessary, add salt and pepper as needed. Prepare the food and serve it right away. When doing, I like to pour some fresh lemon juice on top (up to you). If desired, top with freshly grated Parmesan

Notes

- Serves 2-4 depending on the rest of the meal.
- I used oil-packed sun-dried tomatoes (I drained the oil). If using dry, add more than 1/4 cup.
- The nutritional information is supplied as a courtesy and is not guaranteed. Ingredients can change, and Salt & Lavender makes no promises as to their correctness.

Nutrition

Calories in one serving: 396 8 grams of carbohydrates 26 grams of protein 30 grams of fat 18g of dietary saturated fat 382 milligrams of cholesterol Number of milligrams of sodium in one gram 425 milligrams of potassium 1 gram of dietary fiber Added sugar (sucrose): 3g 1813 International Units of Vitamin A 11 milligrams of vitamin C Calcium has a calorie count of 232 milligrams. 3 milligrams of iron are contained in one serving.

40. CHEESY CHICKEN AND BROCCOLI CASSEROLE

- prep:15 mins
- cook: 35 mins
- total: 50 mins
- Servings: 8

Ingredients

- 1 tbsp unsalted butter, or as needed
- 2 skinless, boneless chicken breasts, cubed
- 3 cups of finely chopped broccoli
- 12oz condensed cream of chicken soup
- 1 cup shredded Cheddar cheese
- 1 cup shredded Parmesan cheese, divided
- ½ cup shredded mozzarella cheese
- ½ cup sour cream
- ground black pepper as need

Directions

1. Set the stove to 350 degrees Fahrenheit and prepare the dish (175 degrees C). Melt butter in a 9x13-inch baking dish and set aside.
2. Heat up a large saucepan of water until it just begins to boil. Boil the chicken for 5 to 10 minutes, or until it's no longer pink in the middle.

3. Broccoli, chicken soup, cheeses (including 1/2 cup Parmesan), sour cream, and pepper should all be mixed in a big bowl at this point. Make sure everything is well-mixed.
4. Remove the chicken from the marinade and stir it into the broccoli dish. Mix thoroughly. Spread equally in the prepared baking dish with the remaining ingredients and bake for 30 minutes at 350 degrees.
5. 20 minutes in a preheated oven. Bake for another 3 - 5 minutes, occasionally stirring until the remaining Parmesan cheese is melted and bubbly.

Cook's Notes:

- If you prefer frozen broccoli instead of fresh, do so.
- After 20 minutes, you can add any cheese you like.

Nutrition Facts :

Per serving,

- 265 calories,
- 18.3 grams of protein,
- 9.1 grams of carbs,
- 17.4 grams of fat,
- 55.8 milligrams of cholesterol,
- 832.4 milligrams of sodium.

41. CAULIFLOWER "FRIED RICE"

- Servings: 4
- Prep Time: 15 Minutes
- Cook Time: 15 Minutes
- Total Time: 30 Minutes

Ingredients

- Vegetable oil
- 2 large eggs, beaten
- Salt
- 1 cup chopped scallions, light and green parts separated
- 3 garlic cloves, minced
- 1 tbsp finely chopped fresh ginger, from a 1-inch knob
- One 2-lb head cauliflower
- 4-5 tbsps soy sauce

- 1/4 tsp crushed red pepper flakes
- 1 tsp sugar
- 1 cup frozen peas and carrots
- 1 tsp rice vinegar
- 1 tsp Asian/toasted sesame oil
- 1 cup chopped cashews (optional)

Instructions

1. Use a grating disc on a food processor to finely chop the cauliflower. Alternatively, use a box grater or a hand-held grater with large holes for grating. Separate yourself from the situation. (If you're using pre-cooked cauliflower rice, you can skip this step.)
2. In a large nonstick skillet (10 or 12 inches in diameter), heat 2 tsp of vegetable oil until shimmering. Sprinkle some salt on top and continue scrambling the eggs for a few minutes or until they are done. Place on a small plate and keep at room temperature. Clean the frying pan well with a damp cloth.
3. Set the pan to medium heat and add the 3 tbsps of vegetable oil. Continue to sauté, frequently stirring, for 3 to 4 minutes or until softened but not browned. Toss in the grated cauliflower, 4 tbsp soy sauce, red pepper flakes, 1/4 tsp sugar, and 1/4 tsp salt—Cook for about 3 minutes with frequent stirring. Add the peas and carrots and simmer for a few minutes until the cauliflower "rice" is tender-crisp. Rice vinegar, sesame oil, scallions, almonds (if used), and eggs are all added at the end. Test the meal and make necessary adjustments to the seasonings (adding the remaining tbsp of soy sauce if necessary). Serve immediately.

Nutrition Information

- per serving: 273 calories
- 17 grams of fat
- 2 grams of saturated fat
- 22 grams of carbohydrates
- 8 grams of sugar are in one serving.
- 7 grams of fiber
- 12 grams of protein
- There are 1717 milligrams of sodium in 1 tsp.
- 93 milligrams of cholesterol

42. BACON AND VEGETABLE SOUP

- 15m prep
- 1h 08m cook
- 4 servings

Ingredients

- 2 tsp olive oil
- 1 leek, trimmed, halved, washed, thinly sliced
- 2 garlic cloves, crushed
- 4 rashers middle bacon, chopped
- 1 celery stalk, trimmed, chopped
- 1 medium carrot, peeled, chopped
- 1 small swede, peeled, chopped
- 1/3 cup pearl barley
- 400g can crushed tomatoes
- 6 cups of Massel chicken style liquid stock
- 1 medium zucchini, halved, sliced
- 1 medium Desiree potato, peeled, chopped
- 1 tbsp chopped fresh basil leaves

Method

1. Warm the oil in a large pot. Stirring constantly, cook the leek and garlic for 2 to 3 minutes or until the leek is tender. Add the bacon, celery, carrots, and swede to the pot and cook until crispy. Stir frequently for 5 minutes or until golden brown.
2. Add the barley, tomato, and chicken stock, and mix well. Bring the mixture to a rolling boil. Reduce the heat to a low level—Cook for 40 minutes or until tender.
3. Add the potato and zucchini and mix well. Add all ingredients to a large pot and bring to a gentle simmer. Add a few leaves of basil, if desired. To blend, give everything a good stir. Serve.

Nutritional Information
Per serving

- 327 Calories,
- 1368 Kilojoules of Energy
- 14 grams of fat, of which 4 grams are saturated fats,
- 7 grams are fiber
- 19.5 grams are protein

43. INSTANT POT TURKEY CHILI

- Prep Time: 10 minutes
- Cook Time: 20 minutes
- Total Time: 30 minutes
- Servings: 8 servings

Ingredients

- one lb ground turkey
- one cup any stock or broth low sodium
- one large onion diced
- three large garlic cloves minced
- 1 bell pepper diced
- 1 1/2 cups of corn canned or frozen
- 14 oz. rinsed and drained can of reduced-sodium red kidney beans
- 14 oz rinsed and drained
- cannellini or navy beans, low sodium
- 14 oz washed and drained
- can reduced-sodium pinto beans or black-eyed peas
- 2 tbsp chili powder makes mild, 3 tbsp for spicy
- 1 tsp cumin
- 1 tsp oregano dried
- 1/2 tsp paprika
- 3/4 tsp salt
- 28 oz can diced tomatoes low sodium
- 6 oz can tomato paste low sodium
- Avocado oil
- Green onion cilantro, cheese, plain yogurt (for toppings)

Instructions

1. Press Sauté on the 6 or 8-quart Instant Pot and let it warm up until the indicator says "Hot."
2. For 4 minutes, fry ground turkey while breaking it up into small pieces with a spatula—swirl oil to coat. Add ground turkey—no need to fully cook the meat.
3. To deglaze the pot, add 1/2 cup broth and scrape away any browned chunks of meat that have gotten stuck to the bottom of the pot. No big deal if it's true. My 6 quart Instant Pot becomes hotter than my 8 quart Instant Pot while it's on high pressure.
4. You can also use 1 cup of broth if your pan has been deglazed.

5. Mix the diced tomatoes and tomato paste with the onion and garlic and add to a pot. Add the corn and beans and the remaining spices. To keep from burning, don't stir anything.
6. Set the pressure vent to Sealing, then push Pressure while the lid is closed—Cook for 15 minutes on high or manual.
7. Once the pressure has been released, it takes around 2-3 minutes to turn the pressure valve to the Venting position.
8. Serve hot with your favorite toppings once you remove the cover and give it a good stir.

Nutrition

- 292 calories,
- 37 grams of carbohydrates,
- 23 grams of protein,
- 2 grams of fat,1 gram of saturated fat,
- 31 milligrams of cholesterol,
- 494 milligrams of sodium,
- 330 milligrams of potassium.

44. CROCKPOT CHICKEN TACO CHILI

- Prep Time: 5 minutes
- Cook Time: 10 hours
- Total Time: 10 hours 5 minutes
- Servings: 10

Ingredients

- 1 onion, chopped
- 16 ounce can black beans, drained
- 16 ounce can of red kidney beans, drained
- 16 ounce can tomato sauce
- 10-ounce package frozen corn kernels
- 2 x 14.5 oz. chopped tomatoes with green chiles
- 1 packet taco seasoning
- 1 tbsp ground cumin
- 1 tbsp chili powder
- 3-4 boneless, skinless chicken breasts

Instructions

1. If you're using frozen chicken breasts, mix all ingredients except the chicken in the slow cooker insert.
2. Make use of a spatula to mix and include all of the ingredients thoroughly. Stir until smooth and well mixed. Make sure the chicken breasts are coated by tucking them in between the mixture.
3. Cook for ten hours on low or six hours on high, depending on your preference.
4. Remove the chicken breasts from the slow cooker and shred them in a stand mixer just before serving. You can also use 2 forks to shred them.
5. Add the shredded chicken back to the slow cooker, stir, and simmer for an additional 30 minutes with the lid on.
6. Serve immediately with your choice of sauce and garnishes. Add a dollop of mild sour cream, cilantro, shredded cheddar, etc., to spice things up a little bit.
7. Just keep leftovers in the fridge for up to a week in an airtight container.

NUTRITION FACTS

- 198 calories,
- 25 grams of carbohydrates
- 23 grams of protein,
- 2 grams of fat,
- 7 grams of fiber,
- 4 grams of added sugar.

45. TURKEY MEATLOAF

- READY IN: 1hr 5mins
- SERVES: 5

INGREDIENTS

- 2 tbsp butter (or margarine)
- 1 cup onion, chopped
- 3 garlic cloves, minced
- 1 1/4 lbs ground turkey
- 1/2cup breadcrumbs
- 1 egg (or 1/4 cup egg substitute)
- 3/4cup catsup

- 2 tsps Worcestershire sauce
- 3/4tsp salt
- 1/2tsp black pepper

DIRECTIONS

1. Melt the butter in a low skillet until creamy.
2. Melt butter in a small saucepan over medium heat. While cooking, add onion and garlic and stir until soft.
3. Allow mixture to cool for five minutes in a big bowl.
4. Assemble your stuffing by mixing the onion and Worcestershire sauce with 1/4 cup of ketchup. Then add turkey, bread crumbs, and eggs.
5. Place meatloaf in an 8x4-inch loaf pan and bake for one hour at 350 degrees.
6. Top with the rest of the catsup.
7. It takes about 50 - 55 minutes to bake a loaf at 350 degrees.
8. (An internal temperature of 165 degrees Fahrenheit is recommended.) Before serving, remove the pan from the stove and let it rest for five minutes.

46.　　GRANOLA BAR

- Prep Time: 5 mins
- Chilling time: 1 hr
- Serves 8

Ingredients

- 1 cup very smooth creamy natural peanut butter or cashew butter
- 2/3 cup honey
- 1 tsp vanilla extract
- Heaping 1/2 tsp sea salt
- 2½ cups of whole rolled oats
- 1/3 cup mini chocolate chips*
- 3 tbsps pepitas or crushed peanuts or cashews

Instructions

1. Use parchment paper to line an eight-inch square baking tray.
2. Stir the honey, peanut butter, vanilla, and salt in a large bowl until smooth.
3. oats, chocolate chips and pepitas all together (or nuts). Keep stirring even if the mixture appears to be dry at first. Mix well and press into the prepared pan firmly. Spread the batter out with a second sheet of parchment paper, the back of a

measuring cup, and a rolling pin. Slice into bars after they've chilled for at least an hour.
4. Keep the bars cool by storing them in the refrigerator.

47. COCOA ALMOND PROTEIN SMOOTHIE

- Prep Time 5 mins
- Total Time 5 mins
- Servings 1

Ingredients

- ¾ cup Greek yogurt
- ¼ cup + 2 tbsp. milk (almond, dairy, etc.)
- 1 medium banana (sliced and frozen)
- ½ tbsp unsweetened cocoa powder
- 2 tbsps almond butter
- 2 tsp ground flaxseed (optional)
- ¾ cup ice cubes

Instructions

Blend full ingredients until smooth in the blender. Enjoy!

Nutrition

- 471 calories
- 27 grams of protein,
- 23 grams of fat, and 3 grams of saturated fat.
- 16 milligrams of cholesterol,
- 98 milligrams of sodium,
- 1030 milligrams of potassium,
- 8 milligrams of fiber,
- 25 milligrams of sugar.

48. HASHBROWN EGG CASSEROLE

- Prep Time 5 minutes
- Cook Time 45 minutes
- Total Time 50 minutes
- Servings: 8

Ingredients

- 8 pre-cooked frozen hash brown patties
- 1 cup shredded sharp cheddar cheese
- 1 cup shredded Monterey Jack cheese
- 1 1/2 cups of diced leftover ham (about 3/4 pound)
- 2 scallions, diced
- 9 large eggs
- 1 cup whole milk
- 1/2 tsp salt
- 1/2 tsp dry ground mustard
- 1/4 tsp garlic powder

Instructions

1. Set the oven to 350°F. Prepare a 9-by-13-inch baking dish with nonstick cooking spray.
2. Sprinkle cheeses, ham, and scallions over the top of the frozen hash brown patties and cover with a lid to keep warm.
3. Make an egg wash in a big bowl by whisking together the egg yolks, milk, salt, mustard, and garlic powder.
4. Bake for 25 minutes, covered with foil. Remove foil and bake for twenty minutes more to get a golden-brown exterior and a clean knife entry in the center.
5. After 5-10 minutes of cooling, slice into servings and serve.

Nutrition

- 259kcal,
- 4g carbs,
- 23g protein,
- 17g fat, 8g saturated fat, 262 mg cholesterol,
- 660 mg sodium,
- 157 mg potassium,
- 1g fiber,
- 3 grams sugar

49. LEMON GARLIC SALMON

- Prep Time: 10 minutes
- Cook Time: 18 minutes
- marinade: 30 minutes
- Total Time: 28 minutes
- Servings: 4

Ingredients

- 1.25 pounds salmon filets
- 3 medium lemons 2 squeezed + 1 sliced
- 2 tsp lemon zest
- 3-4 garlic cloves minced
- 2 tbsp. extra virgin olive oil
- 1 tsp. kosher salt
- 1/2 tsp. freshly ground black pepper + additional as need
- Finely chopped fresh parsley

Instructions

1. Set the oven to 400 degrees Fahrenheit and drizzle some oil on a baking dish large enough to hold all of the salmon.
2. Mix lemon juice with garlic and oil in a bowl with kosher salt and freshly ground black pepper In a Ziploc bag, place the salmon fillets and marinade.
3. Close the bag and move the salmon around in it to evenly distribute the marinade—permit 30 minutes of marinating time.
4. Put the salmon on the plate and top it with the lemon segments.
5. Cook the salmon in the oven for 12 to 15 minutes, depending on how thick the fillet is. It all depends on how thick your salmon is to begin with.
6. Put a couple of lemon slices on top of the cooked salmon, then turn the oven's broiler on. 3 minutes under the broiler, or until golden and crisp on the top.
7. Serve immediately after removing from the oven and garnishing with parsley.

Nutrition

A 294-calorie salmon fillet comprises 9 grams of carbs, 29 grams of protein, 17 grams of fat, and 2 grams of saturated fat. One salmon fillet has 2 grams of saturated fat. It also has 78 milligrams of cholesterol and 2 grams of sodium, and 815 milligrams of potassium. It also has 75 international units of vitamin A and 45 milligrams of vitamin C and has 42 milligrams of calcium and 2 milligrams of iron.

STGATE 4: FISH AND SEAFOOD RECIPES

1. CRISPY GARLIC PARMESAN SALMON

- Prep: 10 mins
- Cook: 15 mins
- Total: 25 mins
- Serves:8

Ingredients

- two pounds (1 kg) side wild salmon fillet (about 2 kg | 4 pounds)
- 2/3 cup plain breadcrumbs
- 2/3 cup grated parmesan cheese
- 1/4 cup finely chopped parsley
- four cloves garlic, minced
- 1/3 cup melted butter
- Salt and pepper
- Lemon wedges, to serve

Instructions

1. Arrange a rack in the oven's center and prepare to bake— preheat oven to 400° Fahrenheit (200 degrees Celsius). Use a large piece of foil to line a baking sheet or pan. Prepare a baking pan with nonstick spray and place the salmon fillet skin-side down on it.
2. In a little bowl, mix the breadcrumbs, parmesan, parsley, and garlic. Add the melted butter and season with 3/4 tsp salt and 1/3 tsp pepper, if desired (or as needed). Mix the items with your hands (rather than a wooden spoon) until the breadcrumbs have absorbed all the butter (about 40 seconds).
3. Combine the dressing ingredients in a large basin and pour over salmon, pressing it into the top of the fish until completely covered. If you want golden-brown crumbs on your fish, lightly mist it with cooking oil spray before baking it.
4. Bake for twelve to fifteen mins, depending on the depth of your fillet, or until the crust is brown and the salmon readily flakes with a fork.
5. Squeeze some lemon juice over the dish before serving (optional). Serve with a green salad, steaming vegetables, rice, or mashed potatoes as an accompaniment.

Nutrition

The caloric breakdown includes 305kcal, 7g carbs, 27g protein, 17g fat, and 7g saturated fat. Cholesterol is 90mg, sodium is 379mg, potassium is 605mg, and vitamin A and vitamin C are every 3.2mg.

2. COCONUT FISH CURRY

- Prep: 15 mins
- Cook: 15 mins
- Serves 4

Ingredients

- 1 tbsp vegetable oil
- 1 onion, finely chopped
- thumb-sized piece ginger, finely grated
- 3 garlic cloves, crushed
- 1 tsp shrimp paste
- 1 small red chili, shredded (deseeded if you don't like it too hot)
- 2 lemongrass stalks, split, then bruised with a rolling pin
- 1 heaped tbsp medium curry powder
- 1 heaped tbsp light muscovado sugar
- small bunch coriander stems finely chopped
- 400g can coconut milk
- 450g skinless hake fillets, cut into rectangles, roughly credit card size
- 220g pack frozen whole raw prawns
- 1 lime, halved
- cooked rice, to serve

Method

1. To soften the onion, heat the oil in a large, covered frying pan. The shrimp paste, ginger, garlic, and other seasonings should be added together with the shrimp paste and cooked for 2 minutes. Continuing to stir, add the curry powder and sugar. Add the coriander stems, coconut milk, and 2 tbsp water to the sugar mixture when it begins to melt and clump together. Then bring to a simmer..
2. Pour the sauce over the fish and prawns, then squeeze half of the lime over the plate. Recover and cook for an additional five minutes, or until the hake is opaque throughout and the prawns are completely pink. Check the seasoning and, if desired, add a squeeze of lime to the sauce. Serve with rice and top with coriander leaves.

3. DIJON BAKED SALMON

- Prep Time: 5 mins
- Cook Time: 20 mins
- Total Time: 25 mins
- Servings: 5 servings

Ingredients

- 1 1/2 lbs salmon, King, Sockeye, or Coho salmon
- 1/4 cup fresh parsley, finely chopped
- 1/4 cup Dijon mustard
- 1 tbsp lemon juice
- 1 tbsp avocado oil
- 3 garlic cloves, finely chopped
- salt and pepper

Instructions

1. Three hundred seventy-five degrees Fahrenheit is the ideal temperature for preheating your oven. In a little bowl, mix the garlic, mustard, parsley, lemon juice, and oil.
2. Place the salmon on a baking sheet lined with parchment paper, and generously spread the herbed mustard mixture over the top.
3. Bake the fish for 18-20 minutes before slicing and serving immediately, depending on size and thickness.

Nutrition

Dietary Information Per Serving: Calories 249.7kcal, Carbohydrates 1.9g, Protein 30.5% Fat 13.4% Cholesterol 8.7 mg, Sodium 371 mg, Saturated Fat 1.7g, Fiber 0.5% Sugar 0.3%

4. SALMON PATTIES WITH DILL SAUCE

- prep:20 mins
- cook:10 mins
- total:30 mins
- Yield:2 servings

Ingredients
Salmon Patties:

- 1 (5 ounces) can salmon, drained and flaked
- ½ cup dried breadcrumbs
- 2 tbsp minced onion
- 1 tbsp Dijon mustard
- 1 egg, lightly beaten
- 1 tsp lemon juice
- fresh ground black pepper, if needed
- one tbsp olive oil, or as needed

Dill Sauce:

- ¼ cup light sour cream
- 1 tsp dill weed
- ¼ tsp garlic powder
- sea salt as need

Directions

1. Mix the salmon, breadcrumbs, onion, Dijon mustard, and eggs with the lemon juice in a large bowl. Shape into two patties.
2. Stir in garlic and cook for a further 30 seconds, stirring constantly. Sea salt and black pepper the patties before cooking them in the hot oil until they are well-browned and cooked through, about 4 minutes per side.
3. Serve salmon patties with sour cream, dill, garlic powder, and sea salt on the side.

Nutrition Facts

Per serving: 376 calories, 24.5 grams protein, 24.2 grams carbohydrate, 19.5 grams fat, 136 milligrams cholesterol, and 1009 milligrams sodium.

5. SEARED SCALLOPS AND CAULIFLOWER RICE RISOTTO

- Prep: 10 mins
- Cook: 20 mins
- Ready in: 30 mins
- Servings: 4

Equipment

- 11.5 Inch Frying Pan
- Quart Covered Saute Pan

Ingredients
Seared Scallops

- 1 lb jumbo scallops, You can get these fresh or flash frozen or substitute shrimp
- 2 tbsp Butter
- 1 tbsp Olive Oil
- Salt and Pepper

Cauliflower Risotto

- one lb package of riced cauliflower, ~4 cups of riced cauliflower
- 3 tbsp Butter
- three Garlic Cloves, minced
- one cup broccoli florets, cut into small chunks (optional)
- 1/4 cup thinly sliced green onions, keep the green tips to use as a garnish
- one cup Organic Heavy Whipping Cream, has fewer ingredients and carbs than non-organic brands
- 3/4 cup Parmesan Cheese, grated
- 1/4 tsp Natural Ancient Sea Salt
- 1/4 tsp Black Pepper

Instructions

1. Melt the butter in a ten-inch skillet over medium heat.
2. Cook the broccoli florets and green onions in a skillet with salted butter and garlic for about 3 minutes until the broccoli starts to turn brilliant green.
3. Make a skillet full of risotto riced cauliflower and continue to cook until it's almost cooked (about 3 minutes).
4. Stir in the remaining ingredients until well-mixed, finishing with the parmesan cheese. Reduce the heat to prevent the rice from sticking, and continue to cook

until the cauliflower is soft to your liking. Turn the thermostat down to a comfortable setting.
5. Use a paper towel to pat the scallops dry. If you're unsure about sprinkling, use around 1/4 tsp of every salt and pepper—Preheat the skillet over medium heat.
6. Wait for the butter and olive oil to start bubbling before adding them.
7. Cook the scallops for 2 minutes on every side in the pan with the clam juices and butter. Allow for a few minutes of chilling before serving.
8. A generous spoonful of risotto should be placed on a plate. Serve it with scallops, green onions, and melted butter on top if you want to go all out.

Nutrition Details

551 calories; 12 grams of carbohydrates; 23 grams of protein; 47 grams of fat; 26 grams of saturated fat; 158 milligrams of cholesterol; 1079 milligrams of sodium; 686 milligrams of potassium; 3 grams of fiber; 2 grams of sugar; 795 IU vitamin a; 76.8 milligrams of vitamin c; calcium

6. SEAFOOD CHOWDER

Ingredients
It makes about 8 quarts

- 2 Tbsp. unsalted butter, divided
- 1 large onion, finely chopped
- 1 celery stalk, finely chopped
- 1 Tbsp. Old Bay seasoning
- 1 tsp. freshly ground black pepper, + more
- 1 Tbsp. dry sherry or mirin
- 2½ cups of clam juice, divided
- 2 cups of fish or seafood stock or broth
- 1 lb. potatoes (any kind), peeled, cut into ½" pieces
- 1¼ lb. mixed white fish (such as swordfish and/or sea bass) and shellfish (such as peeled, deveined shrimp), cut into ½" pieces
- 8 oz. cooked lobster meat, cut into cubes (optional)
- 1 Tbsp. all-purpose flour
- ½ cup half-and-half

Preparation

1. Over medium heat, melt one tbsp of butter. Cook the onion and celery for five mins, stirring often. Cook for 30 seconds while tossing in Old Bay and 14 tsp. Pepper. Cook, stirring regularly, for approximately a minute, until the alcohol has cooked off, add sherry. Bring to a simmer with 12 cups of clam juice if using. Stirring regularly, cook for 5 minutes or until vegetables are tender. Bring to a boil the remaining 2 cups of clam juice, the stock, and the thyme. Add the potatoes and cook for about 5 minutes, covered and adjusting the heat as necessary, until they are soft.Stir in the fish and shellfish and bring to a gentle simmer for 2 minutes. Discard any remaining cooking liquid before adding any additional ingredients, such as lobster flesh (if using).
2. Pour 1 tbsp of butter into a small saucepan and heat over medium heat while the potatoes simmer. Cook till light blond, about 1 minute, while constantly whisking in flour. Incorporate 1 cup of skimmed chowder broth and 1 cup of half-and-half into the mixture, then heat to a simmer while whisking continually. Continue to cook and move as the mixture thickens and becomes creamy.
3. Return the chowder to medium heat and stir in the half-and-half mixture. Stirring occasionally, bring to a simmer. When done, add salt and pepper as needed and remove from heat. Serve with oyster crackers after ladling the soup into bowls and scooping it into them.

7. CASHEW , CHILLI, AND LIME CRUSTED FISH

- Prep:10 mins
- Cook:15 mins
- Serves 4

Ingredients

- 1 tbsp vegetable oil
- 1 fat garlic clove, finely grated until it resembles a paste
- 4 skinless sustainable white fish fillets, about 140g every
- 5 tbsp lime juice

For the crust

- 100g cashews
- 4 mild red chilies
- 6 fat garlic cloves, peeled

- thumb-tip-size piece fresh root ginger, roughly chopped
- 1 tbsp cumin powder
- 2 tbsp vegetable oil

Method

1. 2 tbsp. Lime juice goes over the fish with the oil and garlic mixture. For 20-30 minutes, season the meat and let it marinade.
2. Set the oven to 190°C (170°F fan)/gas 5 and prepare the ingredients. Mix the crust ingredients in a food processor with the rest of the lime juice to form a rough mixture. Use any kitchen paper to dry the fish fillets before applying a quarter of the crust to every fillet. Roast for 12-15 minutes, or until done, on an oiled baking sheet.

8. TANDOORI SALMON

- Prep Time5 mins
- Cook Time15 mins
- Total Time25 mins
- Servings 3

Ingredients

- 1 pound wild salmon fillet boneless **
- 1-inch ginger grated
- 4 garlic cloves minced
- 1 tsp garam masala
- 1 tbsp Kashmiri red chili powder **
- ½ tsp turmeric
- 1 tbsp lemon juice
- 1 tbsp oil
- 1 tsp kosher salt

Instructions

1. Cut the salmon into three or six pieces after washing and patting it dry with a paper towel.
2. Add full the ingredients to a medium bowl and stir until well-mixed. Taste and adjust seasoning if necessary. Use a tiny silicone spatula to cover both sides of the salmon with the spice paste. Whether you want to let it marinate for 20 minutes or cook it immediately, it's up to you.
3. Place the salmon on a baking cloth that has been lined with parchment paper.

4. The salmon is ready when the top is browned and flaky when tested with a fork. The cook time may need to be set if your salmon steak is thicker than mine.
5. Add a serving of spicy cabbage salad on the side and serve with the cumin rice. For a low-carb option, serve it over cauliflower rice.

Nutrition

A 280-calorie diet contains 5 grams of carbs, 30 grams of protein, 14 grams of fat, and 1 gram of saturated fat. The total cholesterol in this meal is 83 milligrams, the sodium is 112 milligrams, and the potassium is 823 milligrams. It also contains 1 gram of fiber and 850 IU of vitamin A and calcium, and iron.

9. ASIAN SHRIMP AND BRUSSELS SPROUTS

- Prep Time 30 minutes
- Cook Time 23 minutes
- Total Time 53 minutes
- Yield:4

Ingredients:

- one lb. jumbo frozen shrimp, thawed and drained well (I used 16-25 size shrimp.)
- one lb. brussels sprouts, stems trimmed and cut in half
- two T olive oil
- salt and fresh-ground black pepper as need

Asian Marinade/Sauce Ingredients:

- Soy sauce, a third of a cup
- two T rice vinegar
- two T granulated Monk Fruit sweetener or another sweetener of your choice
- Agave Nectar, two tablespoons
- one T Asian sesame oil
- 1/2 tsp. garlic powder

Instructions

1. Refrigerate shrimp overnight to allow them to thaw completely before using.
2. Put the shrimp in a strainer in the sink and let them drain for at least 15-20 minutes before you start cooking.
3. Mix the soy sauce, rice vinegar, sweetener (such as agave nectar or honey), sesame oil, and garlic powder in a bowl.

4. Pre heat the oven to 400°F/200°C, and oil or nonstick spray a large baking sheet.
5. To make sure the shrimp are as dry as possible, drain them thoroughly, then spread them out on a layer of paper towels, cover them with extra towels, and blot them dry with a paper towel.
6. In a Ziploc bag, combine the dried shrimp and half of the marinade/glaze combination while the brussels sprouts are cooking. Let the shrimp marinate for at least thirty minutes.
7. If necessary, thoroughly clean and dry the brussels sprouts. (Most pre-washed brussels sprouts are fine to eat right out of the container.)
8. Cut every brussels sprout in half lengthwise, being careful not to make any of the leaves fall off. Depending on how you prepare it, the individual leaves may be overdone. I preferred the single dark leaves, while Kara found them to be extremely bitter.
9. Bake for 15 minutes, then spread the brussels sprouts out in a single layer on the baking sheet and mix with olive oil, salt, and freshly ground black pepper.
10. After the brussels sprouts have been cooking for 15 minutes, use a colander in the sink to drain the shrimp well.
11. Remove the baking sheet from the stove and spread the drained shrimp in a single layer over the brussels sprouts.
12. Put the pan back in the stove and roast for 6-8 minutes, or until the shrimp are pink and just firm enough to eat. To get the most delicate flavor, use little shrimp and boil them just until they become pink.
13. Turn off the oven, toss shrimp and sprouts with the remaining marinade/glaze, and spray everything with the remaining marinade/glaze.
14. Prepare the food and serve it right away.

Nutrition Information:

The following is the serving size: There are 296 calories in one serving. 13 grams of fat are contained in this serving. 2 grams of saturated fat 10 grams of unsaturated fat 239 milligrams of cholesterol Amount of sodium in one serving: 2399 milligrams 9 grams of carbohydrates 3 g of dietary fiber 5 g of sugar 31 grams of protein.

10. BRAZILIAN FISH STEW

- Prep Time: 20
- Cook Time: 20
- Total Time: 35 minutes
- Yield: 4

Ingredients
Fish:

- one – 1 1/2 pounds firm white fish- Halibut, Black Cod, Sea
- ½ tsp salt
- one lime- zest and juice

Stew/Sauce:

- 2–3 tbsps coconut or olive oil one onion- finely diced (red, white, or yellow)
- 1/2 tsp salt
- 1 cup carrot, diced
- 1 red bell pepper, diced
- 4 garlic cloves- rough chopped
- 1/2 jalapeno, finely diced
- 1 tbsp tomato paste
- 2 tsp paprika
- 1 tsp ground cumin (or whole seed)
- 1 cup fish or chicken stock
- 1 1/2 cups of tomatoes, diced (preferably fresh)
- 14 ounce can coconut milk (liquid and solids)
- more salt as needed
- ½ cup chopped cilantro, scallions, or Italian parsley
- squeeze of lime

Instructions

1. Cut the fish into 2-inch pieces after it has been rinsed and patted dry. Put the ingredients in a bowl and mix well. Add 1 tbsp. Lime juice, 1/2 tbsp. Lime zest, and salt as needed. To assure that all of the pieces are well-coated, lightly massage them. Separate yourself from the situation.
2. Over medium-high flame, warm the olive oil in a large saute pan. Sauté for 2-3 minutes with onion and salt added. 4-5 minutes more after the carrots, bell pepper, garlic, and jalapeno are added on medium heat. Add the tomato paste, seasonings, and chicken broth and stir to mix well. Add tomatoes after mixing and

simmering the mixture. For about five mins or until the carrots are cooked, cover and boil gently on medium-low.
3. Taste and, if necessary, add additional salt to the coconut milk before mixing it in.
4. Place the fish on top of the stew and cook for 4 to 6 minutes, depending on the thickness of the fish. Cook the fish in the fragrant coconut broth until it's done, or longer if it's thicker. It's also possible to bake this to completion at 350 degrees F.)
5. Squeeze lime and taste to see if you need to adjust the salt.
6. Serve over rice with a squeeze of lime and a sprinkle of cilantro or scallions, if desired.
7. If you'd like, drizzle with olive oil.

11. SCRAMBLED EGGS WITH SMOKED SALMON

- Total: 16 min
- Prep: 10 min
- Cook: 6 min
- Yield: 6 servings

Ingredients

- 1/4 pound sliced smoked salmon
- 12 eggs
- 1/2 cup heavy cream
- Salt and freshly ground black pepper
- 2 tbsps butter
- 12 to 15 blades of fresh chives, finely chopped

Directions

1. 2 of the salmon pieces should be reserved for garnish. The rest of the salmon should be chopped very finely.
2. Mix the eggs and cream in a bowl and whisk to mix. Add half of the chives and salt and pepper as needed to the eggs. Set a medium-sized nonstick skillet to high heat and preheat it. Add eggs and butter to a skillet and cook over low heat until the eggs are set. Scramble the eggs using a wooden spoon. Don't overcook the eggs to the point of dehydration. Add the chopped salmon after the eggs have come together but are still wet. Place the pan on a trivet after removing it from the stove. Serve the eggs hot, garnished with the remaining salmon and chives, straight from the hot skillet.

3. Adding a dish of store-bought fruit-filled dainties to your brunch menu, along with the other recipes supplied, completes the presentation of an elegant brunch. Per person, serve one delicate, but cut it in half so that visitors can mix and match the different kinds.

12. FISH TACO BLOWS

- Yield: 4 servings
- prep time: 20 minutes
- cook time: 20 minutes
- total time: 40 minutes

Ingredients:

- one cup basmati rice
- 1/2 cup chopped fresh cilantro leaves
- Juice of 1 lime
- one cup canola oil, or more, as needed
- one pound fresh cod fillets, cut into 3/4-inch thick strips
- one tsp chili powder
- As required, season with kosher salt and fresh ground black pepper.
- 1/2 cup all-purpose flour
- 2 large eggs, beaten
- one cup pico de gallo, homemade or store-bought
- one avocado, halved, seeded, peeled, and sliced

For the cilantro-lime dressing

- 1/2 cup plain Greek yogurt
- 2 cloves garlic
- Juice of 1 lime
- Pinch of salt
- 1/4 cup olive oil
- 2 tbsps apple cider vinegar

Directions:

1. Cilantro, Greek yogurt, garlic, lime juice, and salt go into a food processor with lime juice and Greek yogurt to make the cilantro lime dressing. Slowly drizzle in the olive oil and vinegar while the engine is running until they are emulsified; take from heat and set aside.

2. Cook the rice to package directions in a large pot with 2 cups of water. Set aside after you've added the cilantro and lime juice.
3. On high heat, warm up a large pot of canola oil.
4. Chili powder, salt, and pepper as needed are good seasonings for cod. One at a time, dredge the cod in flour, then in the eggs, and then in the Panko, pressing to coat it. Repeat with the remaining cod.
5. Add the cod to the skillet in stages and cook for 3-4 minutes, stirring once or twice, until it is evenly browned and crispy. Place on a platter lined with paper towels and pat dry.
6. Make a large rice mixture and divide it among the bowls. Adding avocado and pico de gallo to your tacos is a delicious way to round out your entree.
7. accompanied by a cilantro lime sauce

13. CREAMY FISH FILLET CASSEROLE

- Prep Time 10 mins
- Cook Time 20 mins
- Total Time 30 mins
- Servings 4 servings

Ingredients

- two lb white fish fillets (four big fillets approx.) (such as Basa or tilapia or any white fish fillet of your liking)
- Salt and black pepper as needed
- 2 tbsps olive oil
- 1/2 cup onion, finely chopped
- 2 cloves garlic, minced
- 1/2 cups of Clamato Original flavor
- 1 can (12 oz) evaporated milk
- 1 tbsp cornstarch
- 2 tbsp lime juice
- 2 tsp lime zest
- Red pepper flakes (optional)
- Fresh parsley leaves, finely chopped (optional)

Instructions

1. Set the stove to 425°F (218°C) and prepare the food.
2. With a paper towel, pat the fillets dry. Sprinkle salt and pepper on both sides of the fillets.
3. Medium heat is ideal for heating oil in a big nonstick or cast-iron skillet. For three mins, or until the onions are transparent and fragrant, add the onions to the pan and stir to mix. Cook the garlic for one minute, continually turning to prevent it from burning. Add salt and pepper as needed.
4. Toss together Clamato®, cornstarch, lime juice, and zest with a fork to make a thick, creamy sauce. Stirring constantly, cook for 5 to 6 minutes or until sauce is somewhat thickened. Serve the sauce with the fish fillets on the side.
5. Bake for 15 - 20 minutes, or until a fork inserted into the center of the fish easily separates the flesh from the bones.
6. Incorporate the crushed red pepper into the meal, as well as the chopped parsley (if using). Serve immediately with mashed potatoes or cauliflower rice as a side dish.

Nutrition

Calories in 1 serving: 435 18 grams of carbohydrates 53 grams of protein 18 grams of fat 6 grams of saturated fat 139 milligrams of cholesterol Amount of sodium in one serving: 222 milligrams 1 gram of dietary fiber Calories from sugar, 13

14. SOY GINGER SALMON

- Prep: 5 mins
- Cook: 15 mins
- Total: 20 mins
- Servings: 2 servings

Ingredients

- 3 tbsp low-sodium soy sauce
- 1 tbsp rice vinegar
- 2 cloves garlic minced (about 2 tsps)
- 2 tsps grated fresh ginger
- 1 tsp honey
- 1/2 tsp garlic-chili paste sriracha, or 1/4 tsp red pepper flakes
- one pound skin-on salmon fillet* at room temperature, cut into 3–4 portions

- two tsps extra-virgin olive oil
- Chopped green onions for serving
- Toasted sesame seeds for serving

Instructions

1. To get started, arrange a rack in the middle of your oven and preheat to 425°F. Heat for at least 10 minutes a big cast-iron pan or another ovenproof skillet over high heat. The pan must be scalding hot for the salmon to not stick to it.
2. Garlic and ginger should be mixed in a small pot together with soy sauce, rice vinegar, and other ingredients. Remove from heat, add honey, and whisk in chili paste. Remove from heat and stir in honey. Pour out some of the cooked glazes into a separate bowl and keep it there until you're ready to serve.
3. Brush the salmon with olive oil after drizzling it on. Sauté the salmon with the skin side up in a heated skillet until it is opaque throughout. Allow simmering for 3 minutes, occasionally stirring, until the salmon has developed a lovely crust. Use a flexible spatula to flip the salmon skin-side down when it becomes opaque on the sides and begins to become opaque on top. Spread the remaining glaze on top with a brush or a spoon. Cook the skillet for 6 minutes in the oven after placing it there (the salmon will appear a bit undercooked in the center but will finish cooking as it rests). Cover with foil after withdrawing from the oven. Allow for a minimum of four to five minutes of relaxation. Top with leftover glaze, green onion, and sesame seeds before serving.

Nutrition

There will be one serving (of 2) Serving Size: 1 Cup Calories: 338 9 grams of carbohydrates 45g of protein 13 grams of fat 3 grams of saturated fat 150mg of cholesterol There are 1213 milligrams of sodium in one cup of chicken broth. 7 grams of sugar

15. HALIBUT CEVICHE

- Total: 3 hr 35 min
- Prep: 20 min
- Inactive: 3 hr
- Cook: 15 min
- Yield: 4 servings

Ingredients
Tortilla Chips:

- Vegetable oil cooking spray
- Four 6-to-7-inch corn tortillas
- 2 tsps extra-virgin olive oil
- 1/8 tsp kosher salt

Ceviche:

- 1 10-ounce halibut fillet, skinned and cut into 1/2-inch cubes
- 1/2 cup fresh lemon juice (from 2 large lemons)
- 1 cup lime juice (from 3 to 4 large limes)
- Zest of 1 large lemon
- 1 tsp kosher salt
- 1/2 tsp freshly ground black pepper

Salad:

- 2 tbsps extra-virgin olive oil
- two tbsps fresh lime juice (from 2 large limes)
- 1 tsp agave
- 1/4 tsp kosher salt
- 1/8 tsp freshly ground black pepper
- three green onions, pale green and white parts only, finely sliced
- three tomatoes, seeded and chopped into 1/2-inch pieces
- one large avocado, peeled, seeded, and cut into 1/2-inch cubes
- 1 small jalapeno, finely diced
- 2 tbsps chopped fresh flat-leaf parsley

Directions

1. To make the tortilla chips, arrange a rack in the oven's center. Set the range to 350 degrees Fahrenheit and prepare the casserole. Prepare a small baking sheet by

spraying it with a cooking spray containing vegetable oil. Separate yourself from the situation.
2. Use a pastry brush, olive oil, and salt to the tortillas on both sides. To make baking easier, cut every tortilla into 8 triangles and place them in a single layer on the baking sheet you've already prepared. Place in oven and bake for 15 minutes, or until golden and crispy.
3. Mix the halibut, lime juice, lemon zest, salt, and pepper in an 8-by-8-inch glass or ceramic baking dish for the ceviche. Cover and chill the dish for three hours to evenly apply the marinade, stirring halfway through the refrigerated time.
4. When putting together the salad, mix the lime juice, agave nectar, salt, and pepper in a medium bowl. Throw in the green onions, tomatoes, and other ingredients except for the jalapenos and parsley and mix well. Toss until everything is well-coated.
5. Before serving, the salad should be divided into four equal portions and spooned into four martini glasses or salad bowls. Remove the ceviche from the heat and do it over the salad with a spoon. Before serving, scatter tortilla chips on top of the meal.

16. BAKED PESTO SALMON

- Prep Time: 5 minutes
- Cook Time: 15 minutes
- Total Time: 20 minutes
- Servings: 4

Ingredients

- 12 oz salmon fillets
- Kosher salt and ground pepper as need
- 1/3 cup homemade pesto sauce divided
- 1-pint cherry tomatoes

Instructions

1. Turn the stove on to 425 degrees Fahrenheit.
2. Add salt and pepper to the salmon fillets before serving. The salmon and tomatoes can fit in a baking dish with the fish skin-side down.
3. Serve with a thin layer of pesto sauce on top of the fish. Cover the fillets with the mixture, spreading it out evenly. Serve the fish with cherry tomatoes on the side.

4. Bake uncovered for 12-15 minutes, or until the fish flakes easily with a fork when tested with a knife.
5. Serve the remaining pesto sauce over the fish and transfer to a serving plate. Serve as soon as possible!

Notes

1. Use only fresh, high-quality fish when cooking with salmon. You can also use any other type of fish you choose.
2. Making your own pesto sauce is simple, nutritious, and delicious. You can also use pesto sauce that you buy at the shop.
3. Grape tomatoes are another name for cherry tomatoes. Choose from yellow, orange, or heirloom cherry tomatoes if you like.
4. A word of caution: don't overcook. When salmon isn't overbaked, it'll be juicy and flaky. Cook the fish until it reaches a temperature of 140-145°F Residues can be refrigerated for up to three days or frozen for later use. When you're ready to eat, reheat in the microwave. You may collect it in the freezer for up to three months if you wrap it carefully. Reheat until warmed through after thawing overnight in the fridge.

Nutrition

A 222-calorie diet contains 6 grams of carbohydrates, 19 grams of protein, 13 grams of fat, and 2 grams of saturated fat. It also includes two grams of saturated fat and 48 milligrams of cholesterol. It also contains 1 gram of fiber and 4 grams of sugar.

THE END

Printed in Great Britain
by Amazon